Life's Values

Alan H. Goldman earned his B.A. at Yale and his Ph.D. at Columbia. He has taught at the University of Miami for twenty-five years and at the College of William & Mary for fifteen years. Prior to this, he worked at Columbia, Ohio University, and University of Idaho, held visiting positions at University of Michigan, University of Colorado, and University of Auckland, and also a postdoctoral fellowship at Princeton. Goldman is the author of nine books, the most recent being *Practical Rules*, *Reasons from Within*, and *Philosophy and the Novel*, and of roughly 150 articles in epistemology, ethics, and aesthetics.

Life's Values

Pleasure, Happiness, Well-Being, and Meaning

Alan H. Goldman

OXFORD
UNIVERSITY PRESS

OXFORD
UNIVERSITY PRESS

Great Clarendon Street, Oxford, OX2 6DP,
United Kingdom

Oxford University Press is a department of the University of Oxford.
It furthers the University's objective of excellence in research, scholarship,
and education by publishing worldwide. Oxford is a registered trade mark of
Oxford University Press in the UK and in certain other countries

First published 2018
Published in paperback 2021

Published in the United States of America by Oxford University Press
198 Madison Avenue, New York, NY 10016, United States of America

British Library Cataloguing in Publication Data

Data available

Library of Congress Cataloging in Publication Data

Data available

ISBN 978-0-19-882973-7 (Hbk.)
ISBN 978-0-19-285701-9 (Pbk.)

On our 50th anniversary, for Joan, who brings pleasure, happiness, well-being, meaning, and desire to my life (along with occasional argument)

Acknowledgments

An earlier version of the chapter on pleasure appeared in the Macmillan Interdisciplinary Handbook: *Philosophy: Sex and Love*. Parts of the chapter on meaning appeared in *A Teacher's Life* (Lexington Books, 2009). Articles that were expanded into the chapters on desire and happiness appeared in *Philosophical Studies* and *The Journal of Ethics*. I thank those publishers and journals for permissions to use those materials. Neera Badhwar read the manuscript and made detailed and especially acute comments resulting in many improvements. Molly Gardner contributed useful critical comments and directed me to recent sources I had not seen, resulting in more accurate descriptions of rival positions. Various parts of the book were presented at colloquia at East Carolina University and the University of Miami. I thank the attendees, and especially Mike Veber in subsequent communication, for helpful comments. Several earlier versions of chapters were discussed in the William & Mary reading group: Josh Gert, Chris Tucker, Chad Vance, Tucker McKinney, Chris Freiman, and Jonah Goldwater. Once more criticisms resulted in improvements. If any errors were to remain, I would share responsibility with all these earlier referees and commentators.

Contents

Introduction

Are pleasure, happiness, and meaning what we seek in life and what we ought to seek? Many people will immediately answer yes, perhaps equating all three. But these equations, I will argue, are seriously confused. This question may be at the very center of a reflective person's concerns, but we cannot answer it intelligently without knowing what these states are and what their relations are to each other and to our more general personal welfare or well-being. And we must further make distinctions within each category in order to know what exactly we are aiming at or ought to pursue.

We might rationally pursue any, all, or none of these states. It is rarely best to pursue any of them directly. The important thing, I maintain, is precisely to make our desires, typically desires for other things, rational: that is, coherent and informed. Doing so will, other things being equal (or regrettably having to say, perhaps better than equal), bring pleasure and happiness in some of their various forms in its wake. In the chapter on well-being, I will explain just what it is to have coherent and relevantly informed desires.

This book will clarify our concepts of all these states. In a basic or rudimentary sense, to have a concept of something is to be able reliably to pick out instances. In this sense we all know what pleasure, happiness, well-being, and meaning in life are. We know when we feel a pleasurable sensation, or that we took pleasure in the tennis match yesterday. We know when we feel happy, when things are going well for us, and when our projects or relationships seem especially meaningful. But having a concept in this sense is not the same thing as knowing the nature of its object. You have a concept of philosophy in that you know when a book is philosophical; but, even if you are a philosopher, are you confident that you can adequately define what philosophy is? Knowing when you feel happy is not the same as knowing what happiness is. The reflective person who is at all philosophically inclined will surely want to know the nature of these states that are for many people so centrally desired, so intimately connected to a good life. That knowledge is what I, after a full lifetime in philosophy (who but a geezer to write on meaning in life?), promise here.

The chapters to follow are similar in structure. Each will critique currently popular philosophical accounts of the topics addressed. Each will defend an analysis that avoids objections to these accounts and to earlier relatives of my accounts. Each will show the relations between its target concept—pleasure, happiness, well-being, or meaning—and motivation and value. Most of us are motivated to pursue pleasure, happiness, and meaning; we typically value them, but not exclusively. Well-being, by contrast, is the all-inclusive category of personal value, what by definition we must, if rational, be motivated to pursue. The complex relations between these four categories will be a major topic of this book.

One criterion I will employ to judge the acceptability of an analysis is that it capture a main use of the concept instead of simply changing the subject. If we are told, for example, that a meaningful life is simply a valuable life, that does not seem to capture any ordinary sense of meaning: at best, it questionably posits an extensional equivalence. A second criterion for an acceptable analysis is that it relate the concept in recognizable ways to others in the conceptual vicinity. If happiness and pleasure, or happiness and well-being are not simply equivalent, we want to know the relations between them.

A third criterion applies specifically to the concepts under discussion here: that an analysis indicate why and how we are motivated to pursue the states in question. We want to have pleasure, be happy, and to rank high in well-being, but it is necessary to clarify the conceptual connections, if any, between these states and our motivations. I will claim that only well-being exemplifies the closest possible relation, in that well-being consists simply in the satisfaction of our central rational desires. The connection between pleasure and motivation, by contrast, is far more complex than hedonists claim (the claim that pleasure is always our final end). Correctly describing that complex relation, in part conceptual and in part empirical, depends on making the proper distinctions within the category of pleasure itself.

These sections on motivation and value in each chapter will serve to unify this text not only formally, but substantively as well, since one major theme I will pursue is the search for what has ultimate subjective value and what we must rationally be motivated to pursue. As indicated, I believe only personal welfare or well-being fits this bill, although pleasure, happiness, and meaning are typical sources or constituents of well-being. Since I will argue as a second theme that none of these states is reducible to any of the others, the accounts to be defended will not together be as unified as reductionist accounts that reduce happiness to pleasure or well-being to happiness.

In the first chapter, I will distinguish three irreducible types or senses of pleasure, each having its opposite in a distinct type of pain. Denying that pleasure and pain are opposites on the same scale, as is now common among both philosophers and psychologists, results from contrasting one sense of pleasure with a different sense of pain. Each of these irreducibly distinct types of pleasure bears a distinct relation to typical motivation or desire and to well-being. In some areas of activity, especially relating to food and sex, we directly desire sensory pleasures, but, unless we are Don Juan or Falstaff, these will make up only a small percentage of our objects of desire. Pleasure in another (intentional) sense, taking pleasure in various objects and activities, or having pleasant thoughts about them, by contrast, enters conceptually as a constituent of desire. Desiring something is in part having pleasant thoughts about it. The chapter on pleasure will clarify these relations, as well as describe yet a third irreducible sense of pleasure that is merely a byproduct of satisfying desires for other things. All three distinct types of pleasure can be very partial causes as well as more typical effects of well-being or personal welfare.

In the chapter on happiness, I will argue that happiness in its primary sense is an emotion having a multi-component structure, including physical symptoms, judgment, sensation, and behavioral-dispositional components, similar to other emotions. Other parallels with other emotions will be noted as well, including the phenomenon of adaptation (tendency to return to baseline levels), borderline instances, and the so-called paradox of happiness (pursuing it directly tends to be self-defeating), which again will be seen as one instance of a more general emotional phenomenon. Recognizing happiness as an emotion captures what earlier analyses got right while discouraging the temptation to exaggerate its place in overall well-being or personal value.

Like pleasure, happiness is at once a source, an effect, and a partial constituent, but certainly not the whole, of well-being. Unlike pleasure, it also contains an implicit judgment of the level of well-being. That judgment can be mistaken, and then happiness and well-being will come apart. A self-deceptive person can be made happy by overestimating her level of well-being, but we may well not want to be that person. And we are not, as many philosophers and social scientists believe, always somewhere on a scale of happiness, since we are not so often in this emotional state, any more than we are always experiencing other emotions. We are, by contrast, always at a certain level of well-being since some of our central desires are being satisfied and some frustrated or postponed at any given time.

In its secondary uses "happiness" can also refer to a mood or temperament, states related to emotions as higher order dispositions. Moods are dispositions to be in certain emotional states, while temperaments are dispositions to be in certain moods. Emotions divide into basic ones, such as anger and fear, and more cognitively elaborated ones, such as pride and jealousy, and happiness. Emotions must also be distinguished from related states, such as attitudes. It will be important to keep these distinctions in mind in order to locate the place of happiness in a more general account of well-being.

As mentioned, well-being is the all-inclusive category of personal value or welfare. The chapter on well-being will defend a desire satisfaction account against the main alternatives: hedonism (identifying well-being with a balance of pleasure), perfectionism (identifying well-being with the full development of human capacities), and objective list accounts (specifying objective sources of well-being). All these other accounts, I shall argue, tend to collapse into some version of a desire satisfaction account. My analysis in terms of desire satisfaction, by contrast, will avoid common objections to this type of account. The objections include reference to desires whose satisfaction does not add to personal welfare (the claim that desire satisfaction is not sufficient for well-being), and objectives we must purportedly pursue whether we desire them or not (the claim that desire satisfaction is not necessary for well-being). Much of the response to these objections rests on the restriction of well-being to the known satisfaction of central rational desires, along with analyses of depth and rationality of desires.

Equating well-being with happiness or pleasure focuses on sources of well-being instead of revealing what it is. And it focuses on only one source, ignoring countless possible others. Once we see what well-being is—the known satisfaction of our central rational desires—we see also that possible sources are almost limitless. Since individuals' rational desires differ, it is not possible to tell them how to live their lives so as to maximize their personal welfare or well-being (but don't stop reading here). Any book that purports to do so is a fraud. It will either tell people to pursue what most people are already pursuing, or it will tell them to pursue what they do not desire and what will therefore not add to their personal welfare. And, as John Stuart Mill famously argued, most people know how to achieve their aims better than do strangers who would interfere.

The final chapter on meaning in life will argue that there is a perfectly common concept of meaning in which to cast the analysis of meaning in life, and that this concept once more captures an important element of well-being for most people. Meaning in this sense is always a three-term relation: something means something else to someone. Lives are meaningful when events within them bear such relations, partly temporal and causal, partly interpretive. Events bear such relations when they cohere within intelligible narratives. This account, in terms of narratively intelligible relations among events in lives, shows why individuals pursue meaning but differ in the value they attach to it. As part of this account, I will clarify the nature of narratives and the type of understanding they provide under interpretation, as well as clarifying the relevant differences between fictional and real life narratives.

An appendix on the nature of desire both parallels my analysis of emotions in the chapter on happiness and further clarifies the analysis of well-being in terms of the satisfaction of rational desires. The concept of desire, like that of emotion, is a cluster concept, defined in terms of criterial properties of paradigms, properties that are neither singly necessary nor sufficient for being a member of the relevant class, but that count conceptually toward inclusion in the class.

This brief outline is intended only to motivate you to read on. I cannot motivate you by claiming that you will thereby learn how to lead a better life (although reading a philosophy book is probably better than some other things you could be doing with your time). I will not advise you on which objectives to pursue and which to avoid (don't pursue fame and fortune, as too many academics tell us, but as I will tell you also only if I assume it's a zero sum game between you and me). To advise you on how to lead your life I would have to know you and your present motivations better than you know yourself, and I'm guessing that I don't know you at all (I hope that more than those I know personally are reading this). There are plenty of pop psychology and a few purported philosophy books with partially similar titles that will so advise you, explicitly or implicitly. This book will not compete with them, but it might save you the time of reading them.

Pleasure

Musical Prelude

Kierkegaard on Don Giovanni

Søren Kierkegaard, in his guise as an aesthete who places aesthetic or sensory pleasures above all other values, claims that Mozart's *Don Giovanni* is the one perfect work of art.[1] It is unique in completely satisfying the goal of all artworks: the perfect union of form and content. The content centers around the famous (or infamous) main character Don Juan, the erotic genius whose sole motivation is sexual conquest, the relentless pursuit of sensuous pleasure. According to Kierkegaard, Mozart's music is uniquely suited to conveying such content, which indeed can only be adequately expressed in music. The sensuous aspect of language is always subordinated to the meanings conveyed, while the sensuous sound of music, its immediately felt sensory pleasure, is its essence. This essence gives music a kind of demonic power over us, just as Don Giovanni exercises such power over all with whom he comes into contact (excluding the spirit of the Commandant, who, as pure spirit, excludes the power of the sensuous).

Kierkegaard contrasts Don Giovanni with two other erotic characters in Mozart's operas: Cherubino in *The Marriage of Figaro*, a boy character sung by a female, in whom erotic desire awakens but is not yet focused; and Papageno in *The Magic Flute*, who cheerfully seeks an ethical satisfaction of his desire in a wife. In contrast to them, only Don Giovanni "is the expression for the demonic determined as the sensuous ... and the expression for Don Giovanni is again exclusively musical."[2] Don Giovanni's sensuous pleasure exists only in the moment, as does the

[1] Kierkegaard (1959).   [2] Kierkegaard (1959), pp. 84, 89.

immediate sensuous power of music, even though both the music and the character are temporally extended. What Kierkegaard calls "psychical love" continues and develops over time, while Don Giovanni's intense immediate pleasures are evanescent although endlessly repeated, an immediacy once more conveyed only through music. What is perfectly expressed is the motivating power of sensuous pleasure, the passion and power of biological life itself, "infinite power which nothing can withstand."[3] Great music, like Don Giovanni, has this immediate emotional impact, the irresistible force of intense sensuous pleasure, the perfect union of form or medium and content in this one perfect work of art.

Complexities

I shall not dispute Kierkegaard's evaluation of *Don Giovanni* here, for I too know of no better opera, but I will argue that matters are more complex both with appreciation of operatic music and with the nature of pleasure itself. In brief regard to the former, appreciation of music is only very partially constituted by the immediate sensuous pleasure of the beauty of the tones at any moment. There is pleasure indeed in hearing the tone of Leontyne Price's magnificent voice or Jascha Heifitz's violin,[4] but appreciation of music and the pleasure involved in such appreciation is far more complex than that, far more than merely momentary pleasant sensations, no matter how intensely pleasurable those sensations might be. Full engagement with a musical piece includes appreciation of its repeated and varied extended melodic themes and its tonal structure, often felt as building tension and release in return to the tonic key.

To appreciate music one must come to it with expectations of auditory progressions, both natural or innate and derived from prior experience or knowledge of particular styles and genres. These expectations are typically fulfilled by tonal pieces after variation and delay, and part of the pleasure of listening to such pieces lies in such anticipation and fulfillment, in having satisfactorily met the challenge presented to one's perceptual, cognitive, and emotional faculties. Pleasurable appreciation of opera involves, in addition, an understanding of the relation of the words or dramatic themes to the music—exemplified in Kierkegaard's

---

[3] Kierkegaard (1959), p. 105.

[4] When an admirer praised the tone of his violin, Heifitz is said to have held it up to his ear and said, "I hear nothing." (Of course he was pointing out where the credit really lay.)

discussion of Mozart's opera—a grasp of the relations of the particular events at any given point to the broader drama, and of the composer's music to his other works and those of other composers. Such full appreciative engagement is indeed pleasurable, but not in the simple sense of immediate sensory pleasure, however intense—the sort of pleasure emphasized by Kierkegaard (as the aesthete character) and sought by Don Giovanni.

Nor is the character of Don Giovanni, his significance for us, simply the embodiment of the successful quest for pleasurable sensations alone. Sensuous pleasure is indeed fundamental to sex, Don Giovanni's main concern, as it is to food (no accident the central banquet scenes in the opera), but it is not a matter of raw sensation alone or independent of understanding of the broader context. Even the sensations themselves, let alone the pleasure we take in them, depend on the broader context and the subject's cognitive grasp of it. For us mere humans, as opposed to Don Giovanni, it makes a great deal of difference whether our sexual partners are beautiful or ugly, strangers or our wives or their twin sisters.

A caress from a rapist is not typically pleasurable, whether or not the sensation in itself is the same as a caress from one's spouse (an interesting question nevertheless). It is the same with the simple pleasures of food (not always so simple, as many tastes in food are acquired rather than natural) or the more complex appreciation of artworks. A cutlet made from worms might taste the same as one made from veal to the uninformed, but certainly not to one who knows the source. Some people find the source and taste of recycled water nauseating, even if told it is perfectly clean and even if they could not distinguish it in a blind test. A painting by Van Gogh can look better than a known forgery, and in any case will give more pleasure in being viewed. The flesh tones of a Titian or Renoir are more beautiful, more visually pleasurable, in the knowledge that they are flesh tones. On a flag they might not be beautiful at all.[5]

To Don Giovanni, as opposed to us, it makes no difference where or with whom he finds his sexual pleasure. His 1,003 conquests in Spain alone make up every conceivable variation in sexual partners, as

---

[5] Similar points and some of the examples come from Bloom (2010).

Leporello informs us in his most famous aria. His master is after only pure sensuous pleasure, and to him, unlike to us, the context matters not. But the appeal of the character to us is not limited to our admiring his erotic genius and sexual conquests. Equally (if equally perversely) appealing is his total freedom from and disdain for social convention and moral restraint, his bravado and total lack of fear in facing even super-natural force. (Mozart and Da Ponte must rein in this perverse appeal by having him dragged down to hell, much to the celebration of the other characters, however anti-climactic.) Mozart's glorious music is as reflect-ive or expressive of these traits as it is of erotic sensuality.

Preview

The moral we should draw from this brief response to Kierkegaard's analysis of Mozart's great opera[6] concerns the hinted at complexity of pleasure itself, at least of our pleasures as opposed to Don Giovanni's (the character, not the opera). I have already indicated two distinct kinds of pleasure: the purely sensory kind and the pleasure we take in pleas-urable sensations themselves and in countless other objects and activ-ities. The next section will analyze in detail the nature of these different types of pleasure, as well as a third yet distinct kind. The history of discussions of pleasure by philosophers first emphasized the purely sensory kind, and recently the intentional kind that takes an object, to the extent of denying the former or falsely reducing it to the latter. (An intentional attitude is one that is always directed at an object. Thus belief is an intentional attitude because one cannot just believe, but must believe something. Similarly, one takes pleasure in some object or activ-ity.) Recent discussions by psychologists and neuroscientists do not clearly distinguish these three types that I will claim to be distinct although related. In that section I will defend another claim that is now often denied: that pleasure in its several senses has direct opposites in pain. In regard to all three types we can place pleasure and pain at opposite ends of the same scale.

The fourth section will examine the role of pleasure in motivation. Psychological hedonism, a position with a long history in philosophy,

---

[6] Remember it is Kierkegaard's character of the aesthete; the philosopher himself is intentionally superficial here.

claims that pleasure is the only thing desired for itself, the only ultimate motivator. Everything else is sought only as a means to pleasure. The type of pleasure provided by and associated with sex has given this position a bad name, leading its defenders to view such pleasure as a baser kind, merely bodily and animalistic as opposed to the higher pleasures of the mind. But, as noted, there is another major type of pleasure, the intentional kind: taking pleasure in various objects including the sensory pleasures of sex. The real question here is whether either type is the ultimate goal of all desire. It seems clear from examples in which we desire other things that the answer is negative, but it will remain to clarify the true relation between desire and pleasure.

Clearly, sometimes we seek sensory pleasures, as in sex and food, but those are a small class of desired objects. Do we seek the intentional kind, desire to take pleasure in things, or is desire itself a matter of being motivated by pleasant thoughts, thoughts that we take pleasure in? These questions will be answered in the section on motivation. I will argue that there is a conceptual connection between pleasant thoughts and desires, and between finding pleasure and satisfying paradigm rational desires, although pleasant thoughts are neither necessary nor sufficient for having desires.

The fifth section will turn specifically to the role of pleasure in sex. That sex is intensely pleasurable has an obvious evolutionary explanation relating to the motivational function of pleasure. The pleasure of sex leads to more reproduction and the resultant survival of the species. But the link between the biology and psychology of sex is indirect; we do not normally desire sexual partners for purposes of reproduction. In fact the psychology of sex reverses the usual relation between desire and experienced pleasure. While pleasure is usually a byproduct of attaining what we directly desire, whatever those direct objects of desire might be, in sex what we desire is precisely the pleasure that physical contact with the partner brings.

Although the desire for sex is mainly a desire for sensuous pleasure, our biology allows for very wide cultural and individual variation in sexual preferences, in what kinds of sex and sexual partners individuals find pleasure. Furthermore, while sensuous pleasure may be the immediate and most pressing object of sexual desire, and most clearly linked to its biological function, we take pleasure in other aspects of sex as well, such as its intimacy and communication of affection. At the same time there might be biological explanations, relating to survival of genes, for various social and cultural institutions, such as marriage and differing standards for men and women. Perhaps, as Freud thought, all cultures must be partially repressive of sexual desire and pleasure. Nevertheless, attempts at excessive repression from the major religions must either fail or lead to very unwelcome side effects. The desire for sexual pleasure resists extinction or frustration, even if its satisfaction in itself contributes little of lasting value to a person's life.

The final section will address this question of pleasure's value. Ethical hedonism holds that pleasure is the only thing we ought to seek in itself (for others as well as for ourselves), or in other versions, that it is the only thing that makes a person's life good for that person. The falsity of psychological hedonism calls both views into question. If pleasure is not the only thing we seek in itself, it is very implausible that it is the only thing we ought to seek. If, for example, we seek knowledge for its own sake, how could it be that we ought instead to seek it only for the pleasure it brings?

Other moral theories see pleasure as either a partial measure of value and legitimate goal of moral action, or as a threat to moral action. It seems that the moral (objective?) value of the pleasure of any subject depends on the worthiness of the subject to have it, on the worthiness of the object to provide it (the independent value of the object?), and on the subject's not being deceived about the nature of the object. Factoring in these considerations will make the measurement of such values difficult indeed. If in regard to many pleasures we cannot measure their value, this again calls into question the claims that we only seek such value or ought to seek only it.

In regard to the value of pleasure to the person experiencing it, I have noted that sensory pleasure might be a necessary ingredient in a good life for almost all people, but unless we are speaking again of Don Juan, it will be only a very partial component of a good life. As for the value of taking pleasure in various other objects and activities, if it is the satisfaction of one's rational desire for personal goods that makes one's life go well, and if pleasure in the intentional sense is only a typical byproduct of satisfying such desires, then it seems both superfluous and again only partial to count such pleasure as the measure of personal well-being. These issues will be examined in detail in the final section of this discussion.

The Nature and Types of Pleasure

Sensations

The traditional concept of pleasure, which came under attack from twentieth-century behaviorist-oriented philosophers, viewed pleasure as a sensation, having physical causes and locations in the body, but also being a mental state private to the subject who experiences it. Pleasure in this sense is a pleasurable sensation such as one feels on one's cheek when being caressed or kissed, or in one's back when being massaged. No one else can experience one's sensory pleasures, although they have locations in visible parts of one's body. While they have physical causes and locations as well as bodily symptoms such as smiling or relaxing one's muscles, they do not take objects. They are not intentional states as previously defined. I feel pleasure in my back while being massaged, but it is not pleasure at the massage or masseur.

Such pleasures, of the type Don Giovanni and we seek in sex and food, are relatively short-lived and vivid only when they are occurring. They typically increase up to a point and then decrease or turn painful with increased intensity of the stimulus, as when a cold shower turns warm and then hot. As noted earlier, they may depend not only on their external causes, but on the state of the subject and her understanding of the broader context. It is plausible that food tastes different, causes pleasurable sensations or not, depending on whether a subject is hungry or nauseated. It might be objected that the sensations remain the same, the only difference being whether the subject takes pleasure in them (second, intentional sense of pleasure), but it is more plausible that the sensations themselves vary. To revert to an earlier unpleasant example, a caress by a rapist that sends chills down the victim's spine feels different from a caress from a welcome partner. In any case I shall argue that pleasant sensations are not simply those we take pleasure in, but form a distinct class or type.

As noted, behaviorist-oriented psychologists and philosophers deny that this class of pleasures as traditionally construed exists at all. Nico Frijda, a prominent psychologist, recently claimed that there is a consensus that pleasure is not a sensation,[7] although this strong claim is falsified at least by implication by other psychologists. Michael Kubovy,

---

[7] Frijda (2010), p. 100.

for example, distinguishes pleasures of the body from those of the mind, as do earlier philosophers such as Mill, who distinguished lower from higher pleasures.[8] Kubovy divides pleasures of the body or sensory pleasures into tonic and relief, the former deriving from external stimuli (caresses, ice cream, etc.) and the latter from relief of need, tension, or discomfort. Sex presumably provides both kinds of sensory pleasures. If we take sexual or gustatory pleasures as our paradigms, then bodily or sensuous pleasures will also continue to be a paradigm. For Freud, for example, other sorts of pleasures resulted from sublimation of the erotic—less intense but of the same sort and source.

Philosophers who deny pleasures as a distinct class of sensations as described above[9] do so for two reasons. First, they deny that we could learn concepts or terms referring to pleasures if they were purely private sensations. Pleasures must refer to publicly observable states or activities. They must be defined adverbially as modifying certain publicly observable activities (a pleasurable massage as one enthusiastically indulged in) or functionally as what follows from certain physical causes and produces or accompanies certain observable effects (sensations as states of the nervous system or brain posited to explain certain behavioral reactions that follow certain stimuli). Without such conceptual connections between pleasures and such publicly observable phenomena, we could never communicate them in a common language.

There is a grain of truth in these claims, but it does not refute the characterization of this type of pleasure as a sensation, indeed a private mental state. It will be sufficient for teaching and learning terms for these states if some are salient to subjects in certain conditions, and if these sensations have typical causes and effects. These physical causes and effects need not be, and indeed are not, as a class necessary or sufficient for the occurrence of the pleasurable sensations. Thus, when a child tastes chocolate ice cream and smiles and says "yum," his parents can say, "That's what we mean by 'pleasure'." Perhaps more typically the child will first learn the meaning of "pain" when he cuts his knee and cries. He can then be told that pleasure is the opposite sort of sensation. But in neither case are the conditions that are necessary and sufficient for learning the term also universally necessary and sufficient for having the

---

[8] Kubovy (1999), p. 135.
[9] The most famous being Ryle (1949). Ryle was inspired by Wittgenstein and in turn strongly influenced later philosophers.

sensation. Obviously one can fail to find the taste of chocolate ice cream pleasurable and can smile for other reasons. Less frequently, a person under anesthesia can be cut without pain, and one can pretend to be in pain or express fear instead by crying out. And once we learn terms for sensory pleasures and pains, we can report on those that have no typical known causes and effects, such as headaches or pleasurable sensations in an individual with highly unusual tastes.

What sensory pleasures and pains have in common across possible worlds is only the way they feel: good or bad. Aliens in other worlds might never feel pain when cut or express it by crying out, similarly with pleasures they feel and their typical causes and effects in us. And the aliens might eagerly seek certain foods without feeling the gustatory pleasures that we do, or feel extreme pain when bitten by mosquitoes, which they express only by scratching. These possibilities are fully compatible with our being able to tell by its outward signs when another person has a pleasurable or painful sensation that we cannot literally share. These outward signs remain contingently related to the sensations, that is, we can have signs without the sensations and the sensations without the signs. How can we then know that others feel the same sort of sensations that we do in similar conditions? We are all human, biologically similar, so why in the world should we think otherwise? Alternative explanations for their behavior will normally not be forthcoming.

The second reason for denying that sensory pleasures are a distinct class separate from pleasure in the intentional sense (taking pleasure in various objects) is the denial of a claim I made above—that what sensory pleasures have in common is the way they feel. The pleasant feel of velvet may seem to have nothing in common as a raw sensation with the taste of chocolate ice cream. And of course not everyone finds the feel of velvet or the taste of chocolate ice cream pleasurable, although it can be claimed that they feel the same raw sensations as those who do find them very pleasurable. I like chocolate, you don't; the difference seems to be that I take pleasure in the taste, find it pleasurable, seek it out, and you don't.

These considerations lead many philosophers to want to reduce sensory pleasures to the intentional kind: pleasurable sensations are simply those we take pleasure in.[10] Such sensations are similar only in the way that the many and various other objects and activities that we take

---

[10] Feldman (2004), pp. 57, 79–80.

pleasure in are similar, namely that we take pleasure in them or find them pleasurable. The reduction of sensory pleasure to intentional pleasure solves the problem of what all sensory pleasures have in common. If so reduced, sensory pleasures do not constitute a separate kind or type of pleasure. Psychologists who deny that pleasure is a sensation also focus on the intentional kind and would also reduce the former to the latter.

But the reduction, however popular these days, does not work. Taking pleasure in a sensation is neither necessary nor sufficient for having a pleasant sensation. Regarding necessity, we can have pleasurable sensations that we do not take pleasure in, as when we feel very guilty about having sexual relations. If we were as impulsive and guilt-free as Don Giovanni, we might take pleasure in all our pleasant sensations. But I for one am not like him in that respect—I feel guilty when unable to resist the intense sensory pleasure of another piece of cheesecake or helping of chocolate ice cream. It might be claimed that I take pleasure in the chocolate ice cream while eating it and only later feel guilty. But if I am an obsessive eater, I will feel guilty the whole time—feel only bad (intentional sense) that I am having those pleasant sugary sensations. At the extreme end of the spectrum, ascetics do not take pleasure generally in sensory pleasures; they seek only to avoid them. And many of us are simply indifferent to the prospect of certain pleasant sensations. I do not wish to touch velvet all the time, not even if it is right in front of me (would that it were the same with cheesecake).

Conversely, regarding sufficiency, we can take pleasure in sensations that are not sensory pleasures—the sensation of falling, for example, for those who like roller coasters or skydiving. One might reply that for them falling is a pleasurable sensation. But if it is the same sensation that others do not take pleasure in, then its pleasantness cannot equate with taking pleasure in it. And it is clearer that we can find distressful (take pain in) sensory states that are not pains, for example itches. On the other hand, masochists take pleasure in painful sensations, as do athletes who think that their pain indicates their athletic gain. They take pleasure in having (not too severe) pains in their muscles.

Reductionists who view sensory pleasures as a subclass of intentional pleasures do try to address some of these examples. Fred Feldman, who analyzes pleasurable sensations as those we take pleasure in, views masochism as a second-order intentional state. According to him, the masochist takes pleasure in the fact that she takes pain in (finds painful, is distressed by) the sensation she is experiencing.[11] It is true that the masochist takes pleasure in his pain. But the second reduction of the sensation to an intentional state renders the analysis too complex and thereby implausible. A simpler analysis that captures the data is preferable. And the phenomenology points to the simpler analysis. The masochist does not find his sensation distressful on the first level: he simply takes pleasure in the sensation itself, even though it is a sensation of pain. Similarly for the athlete mentioned previously.

One might defend the intentional reduction and alter Feldman's account by saying that the pleasure of the masochist is not a complex second-order intentional state because what he takes pleasure in is not the pain (first-order intentional state), but the sexual arousal deriving from the pain. But masochists appear to find pleasure in pain itself, and not all masochists are sexually aroused by their pain. Their condition clearly indicates two different types of states, one purely sensory (the pain) and the other intentional (the pleasure taken in the pain).

As in the aforementioned case with pleasurable sensations, painful sensations are not all that similar to each other either, for example a burn from a hot stove versus a dull headache. What they have in common is not that we find them all distressful (one might not mind at all a slight pain in one's arm when hitting a tennis service ace, or even a stronger pain in one's legs as one crosses the finish line of a marathon), but that they all feel bad, at least to some degree. It is true again that the sensations we feel might depend on our cognitive intentional states or beliefs, about the sources of our food for example. But this again does not reduce the former type of state to the latter.

Intentional pleasure

Thus we have isolated two irreducibly distinct types of pleasure. We must now clarify further the nature of the second intentional kind, taking pleasure in various objects and activities. As noted, we can take pleasure in very different sorts of objects and activities, so that once more it is not easy to say what all of them have in common, to say in other terms what taking pleasure in something consists of. While it is common although unsuccessful for philosophers to try to reduce sensory pleasure to

---

[11] Feldman (2004), p. 89.

intentional, some also seek a kind of reduction in the opposite direction. They hold that what all activities and experiences of objects in which we take pleasure have in common is a certain positive feeling or "hedonic tone." But if we think of feeling here along the lines of sensation, it seems clear from the great variety of examples that there is no particular sensation or feeling that accompanies all experiences in which we take pleasure.

Pleasant sensations may accompany or be the objects of taking pleasure in—I can take pleasure in having a pleasant sensation, but with many other objects there may be no sensation present. I can take pleasure in knowledge of certain facts, for example the fact that I no longer have morning classes, without feeling any sensation in regard to that fact. And I can take pleasure in certain sensations without there being two distinct sensations present. I take pleasure in the taste of steamed lobster, but there isn't that taste and another good sensation present, just the one good sensation that I take pleasure in.

When I have a sensation of any kind, I am aware of it, but I can take pleasure in what I am doing without being consciously aware that I am finding it pleasurable. I am always aware of the object of my intentional pleasure, but not always of the pleasure itself. If I am completely "in the flow" or fully engaged in what I am doing, which is most often the case with activities I find pleasurable, I will normally not focus on the pleasure I am taking in them.[12] In fact such focus might well diminish the pleasure.[13] Furthermore, sensations are normally short-lived, but one can take pleasure in a state of affairs as long as it lasts. I am not denying that one can have a warm and pleasant feeling when thinking of something one takes pleasure in. But this is a third type of pleasure, to be explicated below, not a sensation localized in some part of one's body. Thus the reduction of the intentional to the sensory type of pleasure is no more successful than its converse.

More common is the claim that taking pleasure in anything—whether an object, state of affairs, activity, or experience—is wanting it to continue, just as being pained by anything is wanting it to stop or cease

---

[12] Perhaps when not focused on intentional pleasure, I might be subconsciously aware of it, but I am speaking of conscious awareness here.

[13] See Schooler and Mauss (2010), p. 246.

to exist.[14] But there are numerous counterexamples in which one takes pleasure in something without wanting it to continue. As noted earlier, we can take pleasure in various pleasant sensations, although, as argued, what makes them pleasant is not our taking pleasure in them. It is the other way around—we take pleasure in them because they are pleasant. Sometimes part of what makes them pleasant is their brevity. The sweet smell of a rose is very pleasant but could become nauseating if overly prolonged. Same with a delicious meal. At a certain point we still take pleasure in them but no longer want them to continue, certainly not indefinitely. And certainly we can want certain states of affairs or conditions to continue without taking any pleasure in them. Those who want to retain the death penalty hopefully take no pleasure in its use. I want my dentist to continue to treat me, but I take no pleasure in his doing so.

We can get a better handle on this intentional sense of pleasure by contrasting it with its close relatives.[15] "Taking pleasure in" is often used interchangeably with "enjoying," but the two are not exact synonyms. I enjoy seeing a horror movie or Greek tragedy, but I don't find them pleasant or take pleasure in them. We enjoy only our own activities or experiences. We do say, "I enjoyed the game," but what we enjoy is experiencing or taking part in the game. By contrast, we take pleasure in various facts or states of affairs. I take pleasure in the fact that I have no morning classes, but I do not enjoy that fact. Rather, what I enjoy is experiencing the freedom of being able to sleep late or eat a leisurely breakfast. And enjoyment does not always take an object: I might simply be enjoying myself, which is not, as it sounds, enjoying the object that is me. But I always take pleasure in some object, state of affairs, or activity, which is what it means to be an intentional state. Finally, I can take pleasure in the fact that I am enjoying something (I hoped that I would enjoy golf the first time I played it and was happy that I did enjoy it), but I do not enjoy that enjoyment.

Nor is taking pleasure in something precisely the same as being pleased by it. I am pleased that the dentist will see me today, but I take no pleasure in that fact. Being pleased at something is considering it good in some way. Not so for enjoyment, and I think not so for taking pleasure

---

[14] See, for example, Gert (n.d.) and Brandt (1979), p. 38.

[15] Crisp (2006), ch. 4, makes similar comparisons to those I make below. I do not always agree with his characterizations.

in either, although some would say otherwise. If we think again of guilty pleasures, the pleasure of my next cigarette for example, I do not think there is anything good about the cigarette or my taking pleasure in it. It is true that smoking it might involve some pleasant sensations, which is why I take some pleasure in it (or them), but I still do not think there is anything good in having those sensations—it is bad to have them. I am not pleased that I have them, although I take some pleasure in them.

Thus pleasure in the intentional sense is not a judgment of desirability or objective value, as some philosophers have claimed. Children can take pleasure in things before they have the requisite concepts to judge them desirable. Taking pleasure in something may nevertheless be evidence of its desirability. This is because pleasure is typically a byproduct of getting what we desire, and desiring something is evidence (defeasible evidence) of its being desirable (John Stuart Mill claimed the only kind of evidence). Finally, taking pleasure in something is not the same as finding it pleasant. I take great pleasure in listening to *Don Giovanni* and Verdi's *Otello*, but I would not describe either opera as pleasant (far too weak a characterization). Powerfully tragic operas such as *Otello* are anything but pleasant, yet we can and do find much pleasure in attending them (at least with competent tenors).

Having distinguished pleasure in its intentional sense from all its close relatives, what more can we say positively about it? We can say that it is a certain kind of pro-attitude toward things, but not the only kind, since I can have a pro-attitude toward doing my duty, for example, without taking any pleasure in doing so. As an attitude it is similar to resignation (negative attitude of acceptance) or simply acceptance (neutral), most like a positive attitude of acceptance. We can further specify what kind of attitude taking pleasure in something is by the ways we tell whether someone else is experiencing pleasure in this sense.

Once more we know when someone is experiencing intentional pleasure by noticing its outward signs (and, if we are neuroscientists, its inward signs). If a person is engaging in a certain activity willingly and enthusiastically, with full attention and without easy distraction, resenting interruptions, wanting it to continue rather than be over with, with a contented look or smile, we know that he is taking pleasure in what he is doing. Once more, in opposition to Gilbert Ryle, we cannot identify pleasure with its outward signs, since one can feign pleasure in this way and can take pleasure also in a break from strenuous activity without displaying any signs of pleasure. As in the case of a pleasant sensation, I can take pleasure in something without wanting it to continue, if part of what I take pleasure in is its brevity. I can pay full attention and resent interruptions because I know I must finish an assignment. And so on. But although only contingently related to the attitude, these signs can suffice for knowledge of others' pleasures. And the point here is that we can identify taking pleasure in as the pro-attitude that is typically signaled by these outward signs (and by the inward sign of release of endorphins in the case of humans).

The communication of pleasure by these signs, like the communication of pain or distress, plays a biological role, as do pleasant sensations. Just as another's pain calls for action to relieve it, pleasure indicates that no action is needed from others to change the environment in which a person is engaged.[16] The communication of pain has survival value in calling upon others to aid in overcoming life-threatening situations. Less obviously, the communication of pleasure prevents others from interfering in life-enhancing activities.

Pure feeling pleasure

I mentioned several times earlier yet a third sense or type of pleasure. This type has the best claim to be called a feeling, as opposed to a sensation or attitude, although it occurs far less frequently than the other two types. I am speaking of the warm glow one feels after a major achievement or unexpected fortuitous change for the better. It can be called a feeling of elation, but also one of pure pleasure. It is akin to a sensation, but without specific bodily location, and akin to intentional pleasure in that it may be considered to have an object (the achievement or change). Hopefully you know what I am talking about here because you have felt it many times after receiving unexpected very good news. What you feel at those times has no specific bodily location, does have an object in the good news, but also feels a certain way, as intentional pleasure need not.

This kind of pleasure therefore falls between the other two kinds, and again is best described simply as a feeling. It is similar in this respect to feelings of serenity or fatigue, again without specific bodily locations,

---

[16] Compare Szasz (1975), p. 203.

although more closely tied to its objects or causes. It is perhaps this feeling that philosophers historically had in mind when speaking of pleasures other than specific sensations, and that may be why we still tend to think of pleasure as a feeling. But, as noted, such feelings, while real, are relatively rare and most often short-lived, as people tend to adapt to changing circumstances, both better and worse, and return to their earlier typically neutral hedonic levels.

Are pleasures and pains opposites?

I have now characterized three distinct senses or types of pleasure: (1) sensory pleasure, sensations with bodily locations but no objects; (2) intentional pleasure, taking pleasure in some object or activity; and (3) pure pleasure, a feeling akin to a sensation, with an object but without specific bodily location. Keeping these distinct kinds in mind will be important for the closing argument of this section, which affirms what was historically assumed but what philosophers and psychologists now typically deny—that pleasure is the opposite of pain, as measured on the same scale. More precisely, all three types of pleasure have their opposite counterparts in pain.

When this is denied, it is often because the intentional sense of pleasure is assumed versus pain as a sensation. Such assumptions or emphases are not surprising, for three reasons: first, differences in language used to refer to pleasures and pains of different types; second, differences in the frequency and importance of pleasures and pains of the different types; and third, differences in the neural substrates of pleasure and pain.

First, as to terms in English, I speak of having a pain in my back, but not a pleasure in my back, even when getting a massage. On the other hand, I speak of taking pleasure in a good glass of wine, but not of taking pain in one turned to vinegar. We speak of things being unpleasant and of displeasure, but not of dispain or of things being unpainful. I take these vagaries of language to lack metaphysical significance (as opposed to the different ways of speaking of enjoyment versus pleasure, for example, noted previously). They can plausibly be held to lack philosophical implication first because they are easily explained by the second factor mentioned above, the frequency and importance of sensory pains indicating bodily problems and calling for action, as opposed to sensory pleasures.

The biological role of sensory pleasures is mainly to promote sexual behavior and attraction to nutritious foods. Other pleasures are much more variable and generally lack biological significance. The evolutionary role of painful sensations is broader, indicating bodily damage that calls for immediate attention. On the other hand, intentional pleasure, what we take pleasure in, plays a broader motivational role (to be explicated below). It is therefore natural that we think first of bodily pains and mental (intentional) pleasures, and that "pain" and "pleasure" in themselves refer most naturally to these different types.

But we do speak of sensory pleasures and mental pains, only in different terms. On the sensory level, while I do not speak of having a pleasure in my back, it is indisputable that I feel sensory pleasure in my back while being massaged, and I have argued that such pleasure is irreducible to the intentional kind. That such pleasure falls at the opposite end of the same scale as pain seems clear from examples. When I step into a warm bath, I feel pleasure in the submerged parts of my body. But if the temperature is gradually but continuously increased, this pleasure is gradually transformed into pain of increasing degree. It seems clear that these sensations form a spectrum on the same scale: that the pain I feel later on is the true opposite of the pleasure I felt earlier.

In regard to the intentional type, while I don't speak of taking pain in the taste of the spoiled wine, I can speak of being pained by it, a pretty close locution, although I have admitted that taking pleasure in something is not quite the same as being pleased by it, the opposite of being pained by something. A more plausible opposite of taking pleasure in, although linguistically less similar, is being distressed by. Taking pleasure in some activity is the same as doing it with pleasure—typically willingly, enthusiastically, etc. Similarly, we are typically distressed by having to do things unwillingly, unenthusiastically, welcoming interruptions and distractions, etc. Again we can measure such pleasure and distress or mental pain on the same scale. The distress I feel at the prospect of grading papers is the opposite of the pleasure I take in the prospect of a spring golf outing. As for the third sense of pleasure, this seems clearly opposite to a feeling of depression, most often when we are temporarily depressed by some failure or unexpected change for the worse.

Neuroscientists tend to deny that pleasure and pain are opposites on the ground that there appear to be different brain mechanisms for "positive and negative affect."[17] They do not distinguish the types of pleasure and pain as I have, but speak of affect or "hedonic processing" or "positive and negative states" generally, perhaps assuming reductions that I have argued to be false on the psychological level, that pleasant sensations are simply those we take pleasure in, or that taking pleasure in is having some sort of pleasant sensation. And the literature I have read mainly addresses neural underpinnings of the motivational effects of prospective pleasure or pain, since that appears to be better understood neurologically than pleasure and pain themselves.

Dopamine was originally thought to be involved in producing pleasure, but is now thought to identify and sustain interest in rewards, which then lead to pleasure.[18] Opioids more closely associated with pleasure itself decrease activity in the orbitofrontal cortex,[19] but prominent neuroscientists admit that pleasure is not fully explained in neurological terms,[20] that the study of hedonic processing in the brain "remains in its infancy,"[21] that it is "presently unclear which brain regions are necessary and sufficient for pleasure."[22] This in itself makes it difficult to draw philosophical conclusions from the neuroscientific data at this stage.

Nevertheless, there do appear to be different motivational substrates for prospective pleasure versus pain, different neural circuitry for positive versus negative evaluations of prospective utility.[23] The differences involve activation of the left versus right anterior cortical areas.[24] These differences are reflected in certain asymmetries in motivations regarding prospective pleasure versus pain: slight positive motivation to approach apparently neutral stimuli (curiosity), and stronger reactions to negative than to positive stimuli.[25] Both phenomena once more admit of evolutionary explanations in having survival value. Do these differences show that pleasure and pain are not opposites? As opposed to the scientists who explicate these neural and motivational differences, I would say no.

First, motivation is distinct from affect itself, although related (in ways to be explained below). Second, positive and negative motivations themselves

[17] Kahneman (1999), p. 12.   [18] Leyton (2010), p. 233.
[19] Georgiadis and Kortekaas (2010), pp. 183, 193.
[20] Georgiadis and Kortekaas (2010), p. 181.
[21] Kringelbach (2010), p. 214.   [22] Kringelbach (2010), p. 217.
[23] Ito and Cacioppo (1999), pp. 470–2.   [24] Ito and Cacioppo (1999), p. 476.
[25] Ito and Cacioppo (1999), p. 474.

lead to bipolar opposite behaviors: approach versus withdrawal, where the one is the negative of the other to the same degree. In the same way, different neural substrates can lead to psychological states that are polar opposites. And even on the neural level, simultaneous activation of these separate systems tend to cancel each other out.[26] Third, in regard to pleasure and pain themselves, even if we feel pain more quickly and readily than pleasure, this does not show that they are not opposite states along the same scale. Psychologically, we take pleasure in the relief of pain and are distressed by the loss of pleasure. Most important, each of the three types of pleasure that we have carefully distinguished has its opposite in pain, as shown above.

Pleasure and Motivation

Psychological hedonism

In the history of philosophy it is almost always assumed, if not explicitly stated, that we seek pleasure and seek to avoid pain. Somewhat less universally endorsed but still argued by such luminaries as Mill is the stronger claim of the psychological hedonist that pleasure is the only thing sought for itself, everything else we seek being a means to pleasure. But if we think in terms of the three types of pleasure distinguished in the previous section, the hedonist's claim becomes difficult to understand, let alone believe.

Although we do sometimes seek pleasant sensations, especially in relation to food and sex, unlike Don Giovanni we certainly do not spend our entire lives seeking such sensations but have countless other goals. Nor do we seek warm glows or feelings of elation, although we are fortunate when they come. So it must be the intentional sort of pleasure that the contemporary, if not the historical, hedonist has in mind.[27] And even historically, the defense of hedonism usually involved the relegation of sensory pleasure in sex to the lower ranks in comparison to the higher mental pleasures that take and derive from other objects and activities. This distinction between qualities of pleasure was central to Mill's classic defense of hedonism.

---

[26] Ito and Cacioppo (1999), p. 477.
[27] It is what Feldman (2004) has in mind.

Is it then plausible that we seek other goals, activities, and objects just in order to take pleasure in them? Two objections to the psychological hedonist's claim arise at this point. The first is related to the well-known hedonist paradox—that those who do seek pleasure in everything they do, whose motivation is always to have the most pleasure they can, end up finding less pleasure in their activities than others do. This is partly because of the psychological phenomenon mentioned earlier of adaptation, probably implicitly recognized as far back as Plato. When we achieve things that we seek for pleasure and initially derive greater pleasure from them than we previously enjoyed, we come to expect them. They become the new norm, the bar is raised, and we subsequently derive greater pleasure only from more expensive (in the broad sense) things. Pleasure, like reward, most often comes from activities or situations that prove to be better than expected, so that as expectations rise, pleasure becomes harder to come by. This is also known as the hedonic treadmill. There is again an evolutionary explanation for this phenomenon of hedonic adaptation. If we remained for too long on a blissful high or dismal low, this would affect our ability to cope with changes in the environment. A relatively even keel has adaptive advantages.

Second, as also indicated previously, we most often take most pleasure in activities when we are in the flow, fully engaged and maximally exercising our capacities. We are not focused on our pleasure when so fully engaged and experiencing such pleasure, not even aware at the time that we are experiencing it. Focusing on the pleasure takes us out of the flow and tends to diminish the pleasure. All this suggests that pleasure is typically a byproduct of objects sought and activities engaged in for other reasons. We do not pursue our goals in order to take pleasure in their achievement, but take pleasure in achieving them because of their other properties that motivate us to aim at them. (As noted above, there are exceptions in our desires for food and sex, among a few others.) Even when we want to do something because we found it pleasurable to do it in the past, it is the activity we want to pursue, not a detachable pleasure.

Then, too, we might desire something that we know will be painful, for example knowledge that an illness is terminal, especially if such knowledge is a means to something else, for example putting our affairs in order for our children. Even when knowledge is not prospectively painful, we most often seek it for its own sake or for its facilitating means to satisfy our other desires, not for the pleasure we are likely to take in it. Not only knowledge, but many other objects are sought for their own sakes or as means to objects other than pleasure sought for their own sakes. The psychological hedonist's claim adds a superfluous motivation to these intuitively clear ones.

Pleasure and desire

We may conclude that pleasure of the intentional sort is not the typical object of desire. But it would be premature to infer that such pleasure is unrelated to desire or motivation. We do not seek the objects of our desires in order to take pleasure in them. Pleasure is not the object of desire, but it is not simply a motivationally inert or superfluous byproduct of satisfying desires either (although it is a byproduct). It is in fact also an element of desire itself in the form of pleasant thoughts about its object, thoughts that we take pleasure in having. There are a number of such elements in desires, pleasant thoughts being only one. These elements constitute criteria for ascribing desires. None is necessary or sufficient, but together they suffice for ascribing paradigm desires. To take an example, my desire to play golf today includes a disposition to arrange for a tee time, a focus of attention on such golf-related preparations, pleasant thoughts about long drives and accurate putts, an evaluative judgment that playing golf would be good for me, as well as a certain yearning sensation, especially when faced with a stack of student papers to grade.

Other desires can lack one or more of these elements (none is necessary). These states remain desires but are less than paradigmatic. For example, I can want good weather today without being disposed to do anything about it; I can want the dentist to see me today without having pleasant thoughts about his doing so; I can want world peace without focusing attention on it or having any yearning sensations; and I can want my next cigarette without judging it to be good. Conversely, any of these elements—dispositions to behave, pleasant thoughts, foci of attention, and evaluative judgments—can be present in the absence of desire (none is sufficient). I can be disposed to do something I don't want to do out of a sense of duty; I can have pleasant thoughts about some fantasy world without desiring to bring it about; I can focus attention on things I don't desire; and I can judge that fish oil would be good for me without desiring it. (Much more on this in the appendix on the full analysis of desire.)

As mentioned, however, these elements are all present in paradigm instances of desiring. That is what makes them paradigm instances. Although the dispositional element might be identified most closely with motivation, the other elements, including pleasant thoughts about the object of desire and its properties, are also motivating factors. Thus, taking pleasure in these thoughts enters into motivation, although we do not desire objects in order to take pleasure in them.[28] (As mentioned and to be expanded on below, we nevertheless desire certain objects like food and sex for the sensory pleasures or pleasurable sensations they provide.)

I have said that intentional pleasure is normally a byproduct of satisfying desire, although it is also one motivating factor in desire in the form of pleasant thoughts about its object. Some philosophers and psychologists define pleasure as the response to satisfying one's desires or achieving one's goals.[29] This won't do, since we can take pleasure in some unanticipated event not previously desired, for example the smell of a rose in walking by it. We can also be disappointed and therefore derive no pleasure from satisfying some desire or achieving some goal. I desired to play golf, but after three shanked drives and irons, five missed putts, and exhausting climbs up hills looking for lost balls, I decide I hate the game. I have taken no pleasure in satisfying my desire.

What went wrong in this golf example? When I desired to play, I was not informed about the rigors of the game, the level of skill and stamina involved, not to mention patience. Being completely uninformed when it would have been easy to learn the relevant information, my desire was not entirely rational. If I had known what it is like to play golf, I would not have wanted to play, not having the relevant skills or temperament (entirely fictional example). Then, too, my desire was not coherent with a stronger desire not to be embarrassed on the golf course, and coherence is another requirement for rational desire.

---

[28] For Freud pleasure was not the driving motivating force, but instead distress or deprivation of pleasure. Pleasure represented a lowering of psychic energy, a lessening of distress or release of tension. This fits well with the pleasure we derive from the satisfaction of bodily needs. But this is only one source of pleasure. We do take pleasure more generally from the relief of distress or pain, but pleasant thoughts of such relief can themselves be motivating, as can pleasant thoughts of other objects.

[29] For example Leyton (2010), p. 231; Leknes and Tracey (2010), p. 322.

If we include in the definition of rational desire not only coherence with other desires, but relevant information, information about what it would be like to satisfy the desire, then it appears to become always true that pleasure derives from the satisfaction of rational desires. My desire to play golf was not rational on both counts, and so it was not a counterexample to this claim. My hesitation in endorsing the new claim nevertheless derives first from the recognition of adaptation and the role of expectation. Satisfaction of routine desires that is totally expected might bring no pleasure. The same is true of satisfaction of instrumental desires, desires for things that are only a means, especially for means to avoid future pain or distress. I derive no pleasure from the dentist's seeing me, although I avoid future pain by having the desire that he see me satisfied (apology to my dentist for harping on this example).

What we can seemingly say then is that it is always true of humans that they take pleasure in the satisfaction of their rational intrinsic desires—coherent and relevantly informed desires for things in themselves (not as means)—as discounted by expectation. Even here I hesitate, first because of the example of a rational desire for knowledge that may turn out to be painful. If such knowledge is rationally desired only as a means to make preparations, then it is not a counterexample. But I am not sure that it is always irrational to seek possibly distressing knowledge for itself or knowledge that might have bad consequences overall. A second counterexample is a person who rationally desires to do her duty even if she and others derive no pleasure from her doing so. Again this would have to be an intrinsic desire to do her duty just because it is her duty, and not as a means to the welfare of others.

If these are genuine counterexamples to the initial claim of the last paragraph, then the most we could say is that we normally take pleasure in the satisfaction of our rational desires. This allows both that one can rationally desire something and get no pleasure from the satisfaction of the desire, and, conversely, that one can know that something would be pleasurable and yet rationally not desire it, for example a trip to the Bahamas when I have more important things to do. But although we don't always get pleasure from satisfying rational desires, it would be absurd to ask why we should want what will give us pleasure, what we will take pleasure in. As a reason for doing something, that will suffice in the absence of some overriding reason to avoid the object in question. And to do something just for the pleasure of it means to do it just because it is desired for itself.

There remain these close conceptual links between the satisfaction of rational intrinsic desires and taking pleasure in that satisfaction.

Sources of pleasure

People normally take pleasure in the satisfaction of their desires. But they desire a great variety of things, differ in tastes, and therefore take pleasure in very different things. Can we make out any order or infer any interesting generalizations regarding the sources of pleasure? Many proposals have been made, only a very few of which can be mentioned here (a sample from recent collections on pleasure). One is that we take pleasure in activities in which we function well or progress toward goals.[30] This suggestion fits with the view of the biological function of pleasure as an indication that things are going well and the environment needs no changing. It is certainly true in many cases, but false in others. I can find pleasure in golf even when I am not playing well and have no chance of achieving my goal of lowering my handicap.

A related suggestion is that mental pleasure itself consists in a sequence of emotions ending on a positive note,[31] as in seeking to learn and then learning new things, accomplishing a goal or acquiring a skill, having one's expectations violated and then fulfilled. Good examples, but how does that description fit the pleasure of relaxing in a pool or hammock? Another suggestion is that we derive pleasure from mastery over objects, from contacts with other people, from feeling at one with objects or other people.[32] Often true again, but as a mediocre trumpet player I take great pleasure in listening to great trumpeters with whom I cannot identify, with whom I have no personal contact, and who remind me only of my lack of mastery over the instrument.

Obviously I could continue endlessly with suggestions for universal and all-inclusive sources of pleasure and their counterexamples. I feel confident, however, from a small sample of suggestions as plausible as any, that we must remain content with a relatively shapeless collection of sources that give pleasure to people with very different tastes. Some seek many close personal relationships; others avoid them. Some like excitement; others prefer serenity. Even when it comes to basic needs like sex

---

[30] Frijda (2010), p. 105.
[31] Kubovy (1999).
[32] Szasz (1975), pp. 191, 211.

and food, there are gluttons at one end of the scale and ascetics at the other. In regard to which sources of pleasure to pursue, I allow my favorite philosopher David Hume the last word:

> We come to a philosopher to be instructed, how we shall chuse our ends ... We want to know what desire we shall gratify, what passion we shall comply with, what appetite we shall indulge ... I am sorry then, I have pretended to be a philosopher.[33]

I have argued in this section first that pleasure is not the typical object of desire. We desire a wide variety of things, and people differ in their desires or tastes. Second, although we are not typically motivated by the thought of pleasure alone, pleasant thoughts about an object are aspects or elements of desires. Third, we normally take pleasure in the satisfaction of our intrinsic rational desires. Finally, that we would find something pleasurable is a reason to pursue it.

Pleasure and Sex

Virtually every best-selling book has sex in it. Even if having sex in it is only a necessary condition for lucrative sales, it is best to include it. Hence this section (if you are not interested in sex, you can skip to the next section).

I have said that pleasures, certainly of the intentional and the pure feeling kinds, but also many pleasurable sensations, are normally a byproduct of activities sought or pursued for other reasons. But sex is different. First, the three types of pleasure come together in sex, and second, the usual motivational order is reversed. While the intentional sense of pleasure is normally most closely related to motivation and value (evidence of desirability) and therefore most widely discussed in moral philosophy, sensory pleasure is more fundamental when it comes to sex. We take pleasure in sex first because of its intensely pleasurable sensations, and even the warm glow that we feel in its aftermath when we have taken great pleasure in it most often reflects the intensely pleasurable sensations that we have experienced.

---

[33] Hume (1985), p. 161.

The concept of sex

In regard to motivation, while pleasure is not normally the direct object of desire, in sex it is. In previous writing I defined sexual desire as desire for physical contact with another person's body and the pleasure that such contact brings.[34] One might infer from this definition that the physical contact is the direct object of the desire and the pleasure once more merely a byproduct of satisfying that desire for physical contact. But I never intended to license that inference. What is desired is precisely the intense sensory pleasure that physical contact brings in sex.

Physical contact with the partner remains essential to the analysis because, as argued earlier generally in regard to sensations, they cannot be divorced from their context. A caress may be the same external stimulus as an accidental brush against someone, but the sensation can be intensely pleasurable in the one case and unpleasant in the other. In the one case the contact was desired for its own sake, in the other not. I take sex between partners to be primary and sexual desire to be primarily desire for a partner. Masturbation, while it may involve similar sensations in the genital area, is typically an imaginative second-best substitute, at least in the case of adults.

Interestingly, pleasure has not been a central focus in discussions of sex by other philosophers (the case is different with psychologists and neuroscientists). In the third edition of the anthology *Philosophy of Sex*, the most popular collection on the subject, the entry on "pleasure" in the index cites only ten pages out of nearly four hundred (aside from my chapter), and six of them discuss pleasure only in a negative context. The contemporary philosophical debate on sex began with two seminal articles (no pun intended) by Thomas Nagel and Robert Solomon that emphasized the communicative aspect of sex as essential: the mutual recognition and communication of desire itself in Nagel's paper, or of other emotions such as love, affection, or domination or anger in Solomon's.[35]

Such analyses of sex as having fundamental aims other than sensory pleasure imply overly restrictive concepts of sexual morality and of normal sex, as opposed to perversion. Any sexual encounter that is not

---

[34] Goldman (1977).
[35] Nagel (2002) and Solomon (2002).

highly communicative, for example, no matter how consensual and pleasurable, is either perverted or immoral. Such condemnation is an intellectualized relic of the older view that plain sex is an expression of our lower animalistic natures, a threat to our higher selves. Ascription of other external aims, such as expressing long-term commitment or serving the biological function of reproduction, as essential to normal or socially acceptable sex results in the same repressive attitudes. And unless sex is intensely pleasurable, it cannot serve some of the other positive functions attributed to it, such as the expression of love or affection. Attributing that function absent the pleasurable aspect, sex becomes that dirty, nasty thing you save for the one you love,[36] as some religions seem to hold.

Evolution and sexual pleasure

Plain sex, with its primary aim of intense sensory pleasure, is of course animalistic, biologically hard-wired, although human sex differs from that of other animals in significant ways. That sex is the most intensely pleasurable activity for humans has, as noted, an obvious evolutionary explanation. Sexual pleasure is fitness enhancing in reinforcing sexual intercourse. The prospect of sexual pleasure motivates reproductive activity, and reproduction is the driving force of natural selection. The biological link between motivation and selection is somewhat indirect since we don't normally want to engage in sex for the purpose of reproduction. But sexual pleasure itself, which is our aim, is a great adaptive advantage in driving us to reproduce.

Of course what was advantageous to survival in our primitive ancestors may not be advantageous to us now, and in an age of overpopulation reproduction might in that respect resemble sugar and fat in foods, at least on the level of the species. And the pleasure of sex is broader than orgasm or sexual intercourse, and apparently broader in humans than in other animals whose sexual desire and activity are more tightly controlled by temporally variable hormones. Sexual desire and pleasure are not linked to periods of fertility in humans as in other species, and areas of the human body other than genitals produce sexual pleasure, as do a variety of behaviors not linked to reproduction (kissing, etc.).

---

[36] As quoted by Paul Begala on CNN.

These can be seen as byproducts of the selection of sexual pleasure for its reproductive advantage.

Motivated by pleasure, humans engage in sex year round, and their sexual activity serves social as well as biological functions, such as lowering male aggression and bonding between the sexes. While sexual desire and pleasure are biologically hard-wired (the clitoris exists only for that purpose), the desire itself is social, a desire for contact or bonding with another person. Biology explains not only our preference for apparently young and healthy partners, but also features not linked directly to reproduction but still fitness enhancing. Intelligence, for example, can be sexually attractive, can enhance the prospect of sexual pleasure (as said by an old professor). Biology can also help to explain various social institutions related to sex and sexual pleasure—for example, marriage as a way to guarantee males' access to females and exclude competition, and a way to afford females protection from sexual predators and to clarify paternity.[37] It also partially explains double standards and the apparent greater interest of males in a variety of sexual partners, including strangers.

Culture and sex

Despite these biological explanations, human biology leaves a great deal of room for cultural and individual variation in sexual tastes and preferences for partners and sexual activities, great variation in preferences for sources of pleasure. Physical stimulation is not sufficient for sexual pleasure. Cognitive and emotional faculties must be involved, and their influence is culturally and individually relative.[38] Cultures vary widely across time and space in their sexual norms, as do individuals within cultures in their preferences and practices. More than biology, culture can influence the degree to which individuals take pleasure in various sexual behaviors. But there are limits against which the most sexually repressive religions struggle vainly. We engage in sex for pleasure, not reproduction, and cultural restrictions on nonreproductive sex seldom achieve consistency, let alone success, allowing kissing and holding hands but not homosexual behavior, for example.

---

[37] Abramson and Pinkerton (2002), p. 70.
[38] Abramson and Pinkerton (2002), p. 113.

All this is not to say that sex cannot have value on the individual level beyond that of sensory pleasure. The communicative aspect can be important, as in the earlier noted communication of pleasure or pain generally. We take pleasure in giving our partners pleasure and seek not simply our own, but their pleasure. In that way sex can indeed communicate affection and love and be better for it. Pleasure itself is more easily communicated physically than verbally. But that sex that communicates "higher feelings" may often be better sex does not imply that sex for sensory pleasure is bad in any sense. Steak is better than hamburgers; lobster is better than shrimp; but that doesn't make eating hamburgers or shrimp wrong or bad. In this respect, as they say, sex is like pizza—when it's good, it's very good, and when it's bad, it's still pretty good.

One could say the same about pleasure more generally, although, as noted, one with a guilty conscience may fail to take pleasure in certain pleasant sensations or even in the warm glow one feels when an adversary is harmed or totally humiliated. At this point we can turn in more detail to the more general question of the value of the different types of pleasure.

The Value of Pleasure

Ethical hedonism

Ethical hedonism historically holds that pleasure is the only thing we ought to aim at. The falsity of psychological hedonism, noted earlier, immediately calls its ethical cousin into question. If, for example, it is not wrong or irrational to seek knowledge when you know it might well be disturbing, we have a counterexample to this traditional version of ethical hedonism. A more contemporary and plausible version holds that the only thing that makes a person's life good for that person is the pleasure she enjoys. Given the very limited scope of sensory pleasures and the limited role they play in people's lives, it must again be the intentional kind that is intended. What is claimed to be good for us in the objects and activities we seek and achieve is only the pleasure we take in them.

An argument related to the one we raised against the historical version is relevant here. If pleasure constituted our only good, wouldn't it be what we always aim at? But aside from examples like that of distressing knowledge, we argued earlier that we do not generally aim at taking pleasure in things. Certainly we don't aim mainly to take pleasure in objects, but take pleasure in them because of their other properties at which we do aim. If these other properties constitute the values of the objects for us, and they are why we aim at and take pleasure in them, then counting the pleasure we take in them as a value seems superfluous, seems like double counting. Not only does pleasure of the intentional kind, having a certain kind of pro-attitude toward things, not count as the only value, or the only thing that makes a person's life good, it does not seem to be a major value, as opposed to a reflection of value, at all.

It might seem that this argument presupposes an objective value to objects and their properties that grounds or justifies the pleasure we take in them. Even if the pleasure itself counts as having some value, and positive attitudes as opposed to negative attitudes like hatred do seem to have some value, this presupposition of objective value is strengthened if we have to adjust the value of pleasure according to the worthiness of the object to provide it. If a life of taking pleasure in great achievements of one's own and others is better than a life of taking pleasure in TV sitcoms, then such adjustments are required. And what are we adjusting for if not the independent value of the objects appreciated?

Thus we seem to be driven to an objectivism about value that once more sees intentional pleasure as mainly a reflection or byproduct when it comes to value as well as desire. Intentional pleasure might have some value, but it seems to derive mainly from the independent value of its objects. On this view pleasure in illusory objects, for example the pleasure that an old man takes in his false belief that his young wife loves him, will have little if any value. And that seems right.

Yet the objectivist who is also a pluralist about value, who recognizes that people find value in very different objects and differ among themselves as to what is valuable for them, is driven in the opposite direction, back toward a subjectivism that locates the source of value in the subjective attitudes we have toward objects, the pleasure we take in them. If I value tennis and philosophy, and you value sitcoms and frankfurters, what do these objects have in common, except that we value or take pleasure in them? The idea that they instead share a common objective property independent of our different attitudes, namely value, stretches the imagination. Am I value blind when I don't take any pleasure in sitcoms and frankfurters? Here the value of the objects seems to derive from the pleasure we take in them rather than the converse. This subjectivist position allows for an open-ended list of objects and activities that give pleasure and therefore have value to people with different tastes.

The value of sensory pleasure

We might digress from the difficult stalemate we have reached at this point in regard to the value of intentional pleasure to consider the simpler case of sensory pleasure. On the one hand, as noted, we do aim at such pleasure in food and sex, and it seemingly therefore has some value for us. On the other hand, aside from Don Giovanni, such pleasure will not be at the center of a rational life plan. These pleasures are intermittent and relatively short-lived. They can be highly motivating in prospect and enjoyed intensely when they occur, but their importance in retrospect depends entirely on the interpersonal relationships into which they fit and which constitute their contexts. They seem to be both necessary for maintaining a reasonably cheerful disposition and outlook on life and yet hardly sufficient for a good life. Most people take more pleasure in achievements and relationships than in sensory pleasures. As noted, even sex can be valued in retrospect and in the long term more for what it expresses than for its intense physical pleasures. When one says, "It was just sex," he implies that it didn't mean much in terms of lasting value. While having sex, intense sensory pleasure is certainly primary, but one can also take pleasure in the social bonding, the exercise of a skilled activity, and the loss of self and one's other concerns.

Although not reducible to intentional pleasures, the value of sensory pleasures does seem to depend on how much pleasure we do or do not take in them. But not entirely, since repressing the pleasures of sex and food might be worse for an individual than indulging in them even without taking much pleasure in them. They often reflect the satisfaction of felt needs and therefore a reduction in tension and distress. Absent guilt, sensory pleasures appear to be good in themselves, although one might question whether we have any reason to pursue some sensory pleasure that we care nothing about. If I have nothing to do at present, need I seek some velvet to touch for its pleasant sensation if I want to avoid irrationality or failing to do what I have most reason to do? I hope not.

One might question the claim of intrinsic value further by noting that temperance is considered a virtue. If sensory pleasure is a good, why isn't more of it always better? Two obvious answers. First, more sensory pleasure from overindulging in sex and especially food can have obviously bad side effects—obesity in the case of food and possibly addiction and somewhat shallow relationships in the case of sex. Second, temperance reflects will power, the ability to resist short-term temptations for the sake of longer-term and more substantial benefits. Like other intrinsic goods, the limited value of sensory pleasures must be weighed against other values with which it might conflict.

The value of intentional pleasure

Let us then return to the quandary regarding the value of intentional pleasure. Objects that we value seem to have nothing in common except that we value, desire, or take pleasure in them. But taking pleasure in a worthless object seems of far less value than taking pleasure in something that is itself of value. The former suggests a kind of subjectivism, the view that the value of objects lies only in the pleasure we take in them. The latter suggests the opposite, objectivism, the view that the value of the pleasure we take in objects depends entirely on the value of the objects themselves. Fortunately there is a different subjectivist position that can accommodate these seemingly opposed intuitions. I will approach this subjectivist position by considering another serious objection to objectivism, an objection arising from the very point that seemed to count in its favor.

Once we have to adjust the value of pleasure by the worthiness or unworthiness of the object to provide it, we will also have to adjust for the deserts of the subject to have it. This is different from the worthiness of the object. Freedom is a worthy object of desire, but the violent criminal does not deserve to have it. And when it comes to taking pleasure in other people's pleasures and pains, we will have to adjust yet again for the deserts of those people to have those pleasures and pains. Taking pleasure in another's undeserved pain would then lack value, while taking pleasure in a deserved pain or punishment might retain value. Some would argue that the pleasure itself is always a good: what is bad in the first case is only that the subject has a good that he doesn't deserve. But the problem with this claim is that there is only one state here, not two, and that state must be either objectively good or bad according to the objectivist. The deeper problem for her is that the calculations now become hopelessly complex.

We would have to calculate such objective values as that of a person's underdeserved pleasure at another's overdeserved pain at seeing an event that should not have caused such pain (was to that degree unworthy). Such calculations are not just complex, but seemingly impossible. Nor is this sort of example unusual or esoteric. If we were to measure the objective value of various intentional pleasures, we would often have to make such adjustments, either singly, or more often in tandem. Does it make any sense to assign objective value that cannot be measured? We seem to have an objective property that comes in degrees but in no precise number of degrees.

If we are to aim at producing such value, we have a property that is supposed to guide our actions, at which we are to aim according to its positive or negative degree, but which cannot be measured and therefore cannot serve as such a guide. An objective property that comes in degrees but in no measurable degrees would be mysterious. An objective property that is intrinsically motivating, or ought to be, is in itself mysterious or "queer," as John Mackie argued.[39] That it is supposed to motivate us to different degrees that again cannot be measured is doubly mysterious. I will note further problems for the concept of objective value in the chapters on well-being and meaning.[40]

The alternative subjectivist view locates personal value not in the pleasure we take in various objects, but in the satisfaction of our rational desires. We have seen that intentional pleasure in the thought of an object enters as a motivating factor in rational desire. And if the desire is rational, the thought of its object will be informed as to its nature, as to what it will be like to satisfy the desire, and the desire will be coherent with others of the subject, especially with desires she counts as more central or important. The satisfaction of the desire will then bring additional pleasure both when it occurs and in retrospect. That additional pleasure will have additional value for the subject to the extent that she desires to have such positive attitudes. Remember that we are speaking here of intentional pleasure, taking pleasure in some object or activity or

---

[39] Mackie (1977), pp. 38–42. I prefer the term "mysterious" because I take it to be no longer politically correct to call properties queer.

[40] For a book-length defense of subjectivism in regard to values, see Goldman (2009).

having a positive attitude toward it, which may also be accompanied by pleasant sensations or an overall feeling of pleasure, both of which are desired by and therefore have additional value for the subject. Thus we do not seem to undervalue intentional pleasure on this view.

What about the intuition that the value of pleasure taken in objects depends on the value of the objects themselves? On the account just proposed, more worthy or valuable objects are those that will satisfy deeper or more central desires, those linked to many other desires that will be satisfied at the same time. These objects will also provide more pleasure in their attainment. Thus I take more pleasure in the publication of this book than I will take in watching my favorite sitcom tonight. The former will satisfy not only my direct desire to have the book published, but also partially satisfy my deeper desires for fame, fortune (Ha!), and understanding or knowledge. The latter will remain unconnected to desires other than a desire for some relaxation.

Thus this subjectivist position, according to which value for a person lies in the satisfaction of his rational desires, appears to accommodate our intuitions regarding both the value of the objects in which we take pleasure and the value of such intentional pleasure itself. There is one further problem in regard to the latter. That is that the value of such pleasure seems to vary with the temporal perspective from which we view it. And, in comparison to the intensity of the pleasure when it occurs, people appear to be not very good at predicting the degree of their pleasure in advance or remembering it after the fact. People tend to overestimate future joys and sorrows, failing to take into account both the broader context that tones down particular reactions and the effect of adaptation over time, or the likely return to earlier hedonic levels.[41] They also fail to accurately remember past pleasures, considering only initial moments or transitions, peak moments, and last moments, ignoring durations of events in which pleasure or pain occurs.[42]

The solution, if one wants to estimate total amounts of pleasure over time, is to count only pleasure as it occurs, counting pleasure taken at the time of anticipating future pleasures (as noted, we do take pleasure in pleasant thoughts about the future), as well as pleasure taken in remembered pleasures. But such estimates will be important only if we think of

---

[41] Schooler and Mauss (2010), p. 251.
[42] Kahneman (1999), pp. 16, 19.

welfare or happiness as the sum total of pleasure over time, objectively measured.[43] And I will argue in later chapters that these equations do not capture our ordinary concepts of either welfare or happiness. The actual relation of pleasure to happiness and overall well-being will be explicated there.

Summary

We first carefully distinguished three kinds of pleasure: sensory, intentional, and pure feeling. Each of these has its opposite in a type of pain. Arguments that deny this most often equivocate between the different senses or types, pointing out for example that (intentional) pleasure is not the opposite of (sensory) pain.

We sometimes aim directly at sensory pleasures, especially in regard to food and sex, but also in seeking visual and tonal beauty. These pleasures may be intense, but they are relatively short-lived. They often reflect the satisfaction of vital needs, and so their absence can be devastating, but their experience in retrospect contributes only a minimal level to a good life. Sensory pleasure is the primary aim of sexual desire, and this aim is biologically hard-wired or selected for motivating reproduction. But in humans sexual pleasure is broader than the reproductive function, and this leaves much room for wide variation in cultural norms and individual preferences. Viewing natural or morally permissible sex as restricted to the reproductive function leads to inconsistencies and unhealthy repression.

Intentional pleasure, the pleasure we take in various objects and activities, has been seen as much more central to a good life. But such pleasure is not what we primarily desire or aim at. We desire objects and activities for their other properties and take pleasure in satisfying those desires when they are rational or relevantly informed. But pleasant thoughts of an object are a normal part of desiring it, and so intentional pleasure enters into motivation, but not as its primary object. We also secondarily desire to have positive rather than negative attitudes, and so taking pleasure in things has some value in itself.

---

[43] This is the view of Kahneman (1999), p. 4.

The third type of pleasure, an overall good feeling akin to a sensation but lacking specific bodily location, and akin to intentional pleasure in normally having an object, may be the most rarely experienced. But as a hybrid between the other two more common kinds, it is perhaps what philosophers had in mind in thinking of pleasure as a unitary phenomenon and in identifying it with happiness. But happiness is not a feeling; it includes a judgment, usually implicit, that one's life is going well. Nor is it what we primarily aim at or pursue, John Stuart Mill and Thomas Jefferson notwithstanding. We aim at our own well-being and that of others, the satisfaction of our rational desires. Pleasure and happiness follow if we are fortunate enough to succeed.

Happiness

Preview

Accounts of happiness in the philosophical literature see it either as a judgment of satisfaction with one's life or as a balance of positive over negative feelings or emotional states. There are sound objections to both types of account, although each captures part of what happiness is. My thesis in this chapter is that we can incorporate sound features of these accounts thought to be incompatible if we recognize that happiness in its primary sense is an emotion.

In the first section of this chapter I will raise telling objections to both the balance of feeling account and the judgment account taken alone. In regard to feelings, neither good sensations nor positive intentional attitudes seem sufficient for a person to be happy, either at a particular time or over time. A person can be in such states and yet not be happy if at the same time she judges that her life is not going well overall. Similarly, a mere judgment that one's life is going well seems insufficient for full-blooded happiness. A healthy person with a good job and family can make that judgment while still feeling sad most of the time. A person who is sad most of the time is not a happy person.

The second section of the chapter will first provide a philosophical analysis of emotions that accords with the way psychologists use the term. Emotions will be analyzed as multi-component states including judgments, feelings, physical symptoms, and behavioral dispositions. Prototypical emotions have all these components; other emotions have fewer. The philosophical category of a cluster concept is instantiated by this analysis of emotions. The features of such concepts will be made clear. Paradigm instances have all of a set of criterial properties, none of which is singly necessary or sufficient for being an object of the relevant kind. In the case of emotions, less than prototypical instances can lack one or more of the criterial properties listed above, shading into a gray area of categorization as emotional states. Emotions will also be contrasted with related states: attitudes, moods, and temperaments. Attitudes are intentional states taking objects, as explained in the previous chapter. Moods are dispositions to have certain emotions. Temperaments are dispositions to be in certain moods.

The third and central section will analyze the concept of happiness as primarily an emotion, secondarily an attitude, mood, or temperament. As an emotion, happiness will be shown to have a judgmental component, an implicit positive judgment of how one's life or significant aspects of it are going. This positive judgment need not be correct in order to have its place in or effect on the emotion of happiness. As with other emotions, there are also feelings (pleasant sensations), physical symptoms (smiling, etc.), and behavioral dispositions (energy, openness) included in the emotion of happiness.

The relation between happiness and well-being will be the next topic. Although many philosophers equate them, this equation is shown to be most obviously false when a positive judgment of one's well-being is mistaken but nevertheless makes one happy. Well-being, I will argue, consists in the satisfaction of one's central rational desires. Happiness includes a judgment of well-being and is part of well-being in being rationally desired.

The final section of the chapter will note other properties shared by happiness and other emotions, cementing the claim that happiness in its primary manifestation is itself an emotion. These shared properties include the phenomenon of adaptation, the so-called hedonic paradox, and the existence of both paradigm and borderline cases. Adaptation involves a return to earlier affective levels after an initial surge of emotion. The paradox refers to the fact that self-consciously aiming to have or to avoid a certain emotion is often self-defeating.

Opposing Views

As noted at the beginning, philosophical accounts of happiness fall into two main camps: those which view it as a balance of positive over negative feelings, and those which view it as a judgment of satisfaction with one's life or with certain important aspects of one's life. The former camp in turn divides into those who see happiness as a positive balance of pleasures over pains, and those who see it as a positive balance of longer-term emotional states or optimistic moods. My thesis is that we can have our cake and eat it too if we simply acknowledge that happiness is itself an emotion and adopt a fairly standard account of emotions in the literature of psychology. We are inclined to find both sorts of philosophical analyses—those that emphasize feelings and those that emphasize judgments—plausible, and we need not choose between them if we accept that happiness is an emotion akin to certain other cognitively elaborated emotions. Nor need we think that the concept of happiness has different senses that divide along these lines. While there are different senses to be explicated below, and differences in scope, the main sense that includes both judgments and feelings is univocal.

Surprisingly, while psychologists sometimes refer to happiness as an emotion, philosophers, with one exception (to my knowledge), do not, although, as noted, some see it as a balance of positive emotions. Interestingly, Robert Solomon, who wrote most extensively on emotions and to a lesser extent on happiness as well, explicitly denies that happiness is an emotion: "Happiness is not a mood or an emotion . . . but an all embracing evaluation of one's life."[1] There will be numerous quotations from the psychologists' *Handbook of Emotions* below. Three of the authors there refer to happiness as an emotion. The *Oxford Handbook of Philosophy of Emotion* contains one mention of happiness in over 700 pages, and that refers to the psychologists' long list of emotions. Equally surprisingly, adopting the psychologists' concept with some philosophical clarification avoids the objections to both dominant philosophical analyses.

Feelings

We may take as our representatives of the first philosophical school, the balance of feelings school, Fred Feldman and Daniel Haybron. The view goes back at least as far as Bentham, and Daniel Kahneman espouses a contemporary version of it as well. But the latter two see the balance in terms of sensory pleasures, and having good as opposed to bad sensations certainly does not seem to exhaust even sources of happiness (although they comprise one usually minor source), let alone happiness

---

[1] R. Solomon (2007), p. 42.

itself. And, on the one hand, one can feel nothing but the pleasant sensation of a massage without being happy at that time, if one is thinking of some recent depressing news while feeling the pleasant sensation (the thought itself need not involve any opposing negative sensation). Thus a balance of good sensations is not sufficient for happiness. On the other hand, one can feel happy about a reduction in pain while still having only a painful sensation. If my dentist begins drilling without Novocain, and then gives a shot to silence my screams, I feel happy about that while still feeling a mild sensation of pain. The happiness does not equate with a balance of pleasant sensations, which is therefore not necessary for happiness.

Feldman instead speaks of attitudinal pleasures, taking pleasure in various objects, events, or states of affairs. As described in the previous chapter, taking pleasure is an intentional pro-attitude toward something, and one can have this attitude without feeling any particular sensation.[2] One can be happy at a time or over time, and be taking pleasure in some particular thing versus a balance of positive over negative attitudes, at a time or over time. Hence happiness at least shares temporal dimensions with balances of attitudinal pleasures.

Haybron finds some of these attitudes toward some objects to be too trivial to count at all toward happiness (Feldman replies that one can be made happy by trivial things). I can take momentary pleasure in the sight of a flower while still feeling depressed. The sight of the flower gives me slight pleasure but does not make me feel at all happy. Haybron sees happiness as a balance of longer-term and more central emotions and moods (to be described below). More specifically, for him happiness is a combination of a positive balance of central affective states and a propensity or disposition to have such positive moods. This disposition lies between moods themselves and temperaments, which are more permanent traits of individuals. Again, in these terms one can be happy at a time or be disposed longer-term to feel happy.[3]

There are telling objections to both these versions of the balance of positive over negative mental states account. In regard to positive attitudes, at a given time one can be thinking of more things toward which one has a positive attitude than negatively judged things without being

---

[2] F. Feldman (2010), p. 111.
[3] D. Haybron (2013), pp. 46, 138, 147.

happy at that time, if one then feels nothing in particular and does not judge that one's life is going well at that time. I can think only of the publication of this book, and while I take pleasure in that thought and will be happy in the future about its publication, I might not be happy now if I currently would not judge my life to be going so well. The same is true over time in regard to pleasant thoughts and overall happiness.

In regard to positive emotions, Feldman finds talk of them too vague, and so he eschews talk of emotions altogether.[4] I agree with his assessment of positive emotions as a class. Are they supposed to be emotions that it is good to have? Presumably not, since it can be good to be fearful of or angry at certain things, and yet these seem not to be positive emotions. Are they supposed to be emotions or moods accompanied by or including pleasant sensations? But which are these emotions other than happiness or its more intense cousins, joy and elation? Possibly pride, but is pride positive when it is misplaced, exaggerated, or constantly expressed? And can't we be in a positive emotional state without feeling any sensation? I can be proud of my past achievements without getting all tingly at the thought of each one.

Haybron speaks of three kinds of positive emotional states that count toward happiness. The first are those of "endorsement," including joy and sadness, which he calls fleeting emotions and deems least important. Second are those of "engagement": being energetic, interested, or "in the flow." These strike me as not emotions at all, but other sorts of mental states or ways of behaving. I am energetic, interested, and in the flow when I am playing tennis, but I might not feel any particular emotion during an ordinary point. Certainly if I am losing, I might not feel particularly happy, however much I am in the flow of the match. Haybron's third class of positive emotional states are those of "attunement," mainly tranquility, which again seems not to be an emotion but the lack of emotions, an inner calm. Feeling calm is quite different from being happy.

More telling, there are again counterexamples in both directions to the balance of emotions account. A person can feel mainly anger at a given time and yet be overall happy at that time if he judges his life to be otherwise going well. My anger at my dean for not paying for my

---

[4] Feldman (2010), pp. 257–8.

conference trip need not override my happiness at the prospect of the trip, although there is no third emotion to override the anger. (Remember that for him happiness is not an emotion, but in large part the balance of other emotions.) Conversely, a person can be drunk or drugged all the time and consequently in a mood that feels good, but retain the sense to judge that his life is not going well, in which case we would be reluctant to call him happy. Or a person could be cheerful in the face of hardship without being happy, if again she does not judge her life to be going well. In contrast to Haybron, I will argue that happiness is not a balance of other emotions, but is itself primarily an emotion.

In regard to Haybron's propensity to be in certain positive moods that falls short of being a person's temperament or character trait, I will by contrast distinguish three levels of affective states: emotions, moods as dispositions to feel certain emotions, and temperaments as dispositions to be in certain moods. I see no need to posit an additional level between moods and temperaments. I doubt that such a category exists in common parlance or psychology, and I don't find a conceptual space for it to occupy.

Judgments

We may take as our representative of the judgment school L. W. Sumner. The primary sense of happiness for him is "having a certain kind of positive attitude toward your life . . . a positive evaluation of the conditions of your life, a judgment that it measures up favorably against your standards."[5] In addition to this judgmental or cognitive aspect of this attitude, Sumner includes an affective component, which he describes as "a sense of well-being," feeling satisfied with your life or finding it rewarding.[6] But feeling satisfied with your life seems little different from implicitly judging it to be satisfactory, little different from the cognitive component as Sumner characterizes it.

Sumner would perhaps reply that the two are distinct in that a person might make a negative judgment if she has very high standards for a

---

[5] L. W. Sumner (1996), p. 145. Sumner also notes two secondary senses of happiness. The first is a pro-attitude toward particular objects or states of affairs, things one is happy about. The second is a pure feeling of happiness, "not quite grand enough to count as an emotion," a "mood of optimism" lacking an intentional object (p. 144).

[6] Sumner (1996), p. 146.

satisfactory life, and yet feel quite satisfied. Conversely, she might feel dissatisfied while judging her life to be satisfactory by ordinary or objective standards (she has a good job, marriage, etc.). But since emotions themselves contain implicit judgments, and the emotion of happiness as I will characterize it contains an implicit judgment about the conditions of one's life, this split will be highly unusual. It would be similar to being in the emotional state of fear while judging the situation to be harmless. This can happen in the case of phobias, but these are recognized to be irrational and not normal conditions. It would be similarly abnormal to feel dissatisfied while judging one's life to be satisfactory. I will describe the affective aspects of happiness differently below. If we take the judgment of satisfaction with life to be what Sumner mainly has in mind, then, as he says, "this identification of happiness with life satisfaction is a theme running through much of the recent philosophical literature on happiness."[7]

Once more there are counterexamples to the claim that happiness is simply a judgment that one is satisfied with one's life or with the way it is going at a time. First, one can be satisfied because one expects no more. If a person low on the social ladder has learned to accept low standards, she can be satisfied that she is meeting them without feeling happy. It is better to describe the (implicit) judgment as a belief that one's life is going well. (Sumner uses "satisfied" and "going well" interchangeably.) More important, that judgment, however characterized, seems insufficient for full-blooded happiness. As Feldman points out, if a person is never cheerful and never smiles, we would not judge her happy whatever judgments she makes about her life.[8] A person who has a good job and family and therefore judges that his life is going well, but nevertheless, perhaps because of a hormonal imbalance, most often feels down and depressed again does not seem to be a happy person. (These feelings need not be described as feelings of dissatisfaction with one's life.) A judgment alone seems too cold to render one fully happy, which is why Sumner includes an affective component. But I will argue that this component, the fact that real happiness also feels good, is different from merely feeling satisfied.

---

[7] Sumner (1996), p. 149. Another leading proponent of the view is W. Tatarkiewicz (1976).
[8] Feldman (2010), p. 3.

It has also been argued that a judgment of satisfaction with life is not necessary for happiness on the ground that a person can be happy at times when she is not judging anything about her life. In fact, as noted, people are often happiest when they are in the flow of some activity and not thinking about anything but that activity and its object. I think that such cases can be handled by emphasizing that the judgment of how one's life is going is most often implicit, as is the case with the cognitive component of emotions generally. But there are other more relevant cases. As noted, a person who is very ambitious and therefore has very high standards for his life and judges that it is not going so well yet, but is nevertheless generally cheerful and energetic, can count as happy.

Thus, we have highly problematic cases in relation to both currently popular philosophical accounts of happiness. I will later characterize such cases, as mentioned above, as gray areas in relation to ascriptions of happiness. By means of such cited cases each side to the debate can nevertheless successfully refute the sufficiency of the other side's analysis. And the two sides have been thought to be incompatible. My main contention is that we need not regard the main features of these opposing accounts as mutually exclusive, as their proponents do. Characterizing happiness as an emotion will include all these features. Before we can offer such an account of happiness, we must explicate the proper analysis of emotions generally.

Emotions

Psychologists' concept

Let us first see how several psychologists have described the concept of an emotion in a recent major collection of essays on the topic from different areas of psychology. Nico Frijda, who has written extensively on the subject, describes the concept as follows: "The concept fits states of synchronization of several components . . . that flexibly influence each other." The "multicomponent nature of emotions entails a looseness of structure . . . a collection of interacting processes."[9] The multiple

---

[9] N. Frijda (2008), pp. 73, 75.

components causally interact in all directions: "Facial expressions that respond to appraisals in turn influence appraisals."[10] For him, emotions include not only bodily changes and cognitive appraisals, but sensations or feelings, and motivations or dispositions to actions that override other sources of action.[11] The cognitive appraisals or judgments are automatic and nonconscious.[12] Negative emotions arise from threats to the subject's concerns, and positive emotions from indications of success.

James Gross defines emotions in terms of prototypes that include judgments relative to goals, subjective experiences, bodily changes, dispositions to behave, and compelled attention.[13] John Bates, Jackson Goodnight, and Jennifer Fite again define emotion in terms of processes including perceptual and cognitive, motivational, affective, and expressive.[14] Another group writes: "In our theory emotional responses are distinct from automatic, affective, and physical responses [but include them], in that emotions require higher-order cognitive processes and encode a plan of action." They note that the rapidity of responses when in emotional states can be matched by rapid evaluations.[15] According to Paula Niedenthal, emotion concepts include appraisals of situations, likely actions, feelings, and physiological changes. These are probable features, neither necessary nor separately sufficient.[16] Gerald Clore and Andrew Ortony speak of "the conjunction of expressions, physiology, behavior inclination, experience." These are constituents of emotions, and not just indicators of latent states (states of the brain). The cognitive activity is implicit, not conscious, transforming feeling by appraisal.[17] Finally, Barbara Fredrickson and Michael Cohn write that a "consensus is emerging that emotions are best conceptualized as multicomponent response tendencies—incorporating muscle tension, hormone release, cardiovascular changes, facial expression, attention, and cognition, among other changes."[18]

I hope the reader will excuse the repetition of the previous paragraphs, necessary to indicate just how common the multi-component analysis has become in contemporary psychology. All these writings are post-Griffiths,

---

[10] Frijda (2008), p. 75.   [11] Frijda (2008), p. 72.   [12] Frijda (2008), p. 71.
[13] J. Gross (2008), pp. 498–9.   [14] J. Bates, J. Goodnight, and J. Fite (2008), p. 486.
[15] N. Stein, M. W. Hernandez, and T. Trabasso (2008), pp. 578–9.
[16] P. Niedenthal (2008), pp. 588, 592.
[17] G. Clore and A. Ortony (2008), pp. 630–1, 637.
[18] B. Fredrickson and M. Cohn (2008), p. 778.

after Paul Griffiths's attack on the concept of emotion in mature psychology on the ground that these components together, as operating in various states commonly classified as emotions, do not map neatly onto discrete causal mechanisms in brain structures or processes. Basic emotions such as fear or anger are quite different in their neurological underpinnings from cognitively elaborated emotions such as pride or jealousy.

As Frijda argues against Griffiths's position, the concept of emotion remains functionally useful independently of whether the underlying physiological processes are unified or specific.[19] Since, as Clore and Ortony also note, the various components constitute emotions instead of indicating latent states, no single causal mechanism is presupposed. Emotions as motivational states, despite including cognitive appraisals or evaluative judgments as components, bypass ordinary rational deliberation. This feature is shared by all states commonly classified as emotions, and it serves their various functions.

This is not the place for a full argument against the eliminativist program. I have argued elsewhere that the lack of reduction to a lower level of explanation is the reason we use functional concepts, not a reason to revise or eliminate them. It is why we speak of actions instead of physical movements, of curveballs instead of particular arcs of baseballs, of guns instead of collections of molecules.[20] There is no unified set of physical movements to which the concept of an action can be reduced or onto which it can be neatly mapped. This is a primary reason to retain the concept: a reason why it is indispensable, not a reason to eliminate it. The same is true of the functionally useful concept of emotions as irreducible to and not neatly mapped onto a unified neurological base.

Related states

I mean here only to endorse the legitimacy of adapting the concept of emotion standard in current psychology to the analysis of happiness. As a further necessary preliminary, we need also to note distinctions in types of emotions and relations to other close states including temperaments, moods, and attitudes, since the concept of happiness applies in subsidiary uses to these states as well. Regarding types of emotions, basic ones

---

[19] Frijda (2008), p. 70.   [20] For more extensive argument, see Goldman (2017).

such as anger and fear are "adaptive responses to particular events,"[21] innate action systems having clear adaptive functions.[22] Fear prompts immediate reactions to danger, as does anger to blocked goals. If I see a large snake, I am better off not pausing to evaluate the danger it might pose. I am more safe than sorry when my fear takes over, however unpleasant that feeling might be. Anger too has an adaptive function, discouraging attacks on one's rights and welfare. Sometimes, of course, one should try to control one's fear or anger by conscious consideration of long range reasons, but one is still better off overall for having such immediate reactions. These emotions, which exist in lower species as well, involve set reactions to an immediate grasp or implicit appraisal of a perceived situation.

"Higher" emotions, such as pride or jealousy, involve more complex cognitive processes presupposing personal and cultural norms and expectations.[23] Pride is a cognitively mediated response to culturally endorsed accomplishments. Such cognitive elaboration, involving cortical areas of the brain, turns raw affects in subcortical areas into more complex emotions.[24] Despite these distinctions in complexity of cognitions and neural bases, emotion concepts apply in both sorts of cases because the structural components—judgment, affect, behavioral disposition, etc.—are the same, and because both sorts of states can replace or override rationally formed beliefs or deliberations (but can also be somewhat controlled in humans on the conscious level). There are adaptive benefits to the more cognitively elaborated emotions as well. Pride in past accomplishments can spur one on to future ones, whether or not its degree is fully rationally supported.

Regarding connections to related mental states, the distinctions mainly consist in occurrent versus dispositional senses. Moods can be defined as dispositions on the first level to be in certain emotional states. A good mood is a disposition to feel happy in the occurrent sense. A bad mood is a disposition to feel negative emotions such as anger or sadness. As dispositions, moods lack components of emotions: judgments and intentional objects, sensations or feelings. If I am in a bad mood, I am not in a bad mood at or about anything (although something may have caused it), and I need not feel any sensation. Temperaments can be

---

[21] M. Lewis (2008), p. 306.   [22] Frijda (2008), p. 73.
[23] Frijda (2008), p. 82.   [24] J. Panksepp (2008), p. 48.

defined as dispositions on the second level to be in certain moods. A person with a happy temperament tends to be in good moods; a person with a sour temperament tends to be in bad moods.

The concept of happiness can be applied on any of these levels, as will be elaborated below, and, partly depending on the level, can take an intentional object or not. One can be happy about certain things or just be happy, occurrently or dispositionally. Emotions generally can be dispositional as well as occurrent. I can fear snakes without currently fearing a particular snake, although I will then be disposed to fear particular snakes. Fear in the dispositional sense will not involve sensations or physical symptoms until manifested occurrently. Attitudes, as opposed to emotions, always take intentional objects. "She has a good attitude" is shorthand for "She has a good attitude toward her work." Attitudes, once more, do not typically involve the sensations or physical symptoms that emotions include.

The philosophical analysis

We are now in a position to clarify the earlier explicated psychological concept of emotion by applying a familiar philosophical metaconcept. By way of illustration and review, we noted that an angry person takes offense (believes that he has been wronged), glares and scowls, feels muscle tension and increased heartbeat, and is disposed to strike out at the offender.[25] A fearful person sees and judges danger, trembles and feels increased heartbeat, feels queasy, and is disposed to flee. None of these components is separately necessary or sufficient, although jointly they suffice for ascribing the emotions. Regarding necessity, I can be angry without scowling, feeling tight muscles, or striking out, if I control my anger. Regarding sufficiency, I can feel and do these things for other reasons, if I am in a boxing match, for example. I can feel angry at nothing in particular, if I am in an angry mood; and I can think I have been wronged without feeling angry about it, if I am a calm and forgiving person. But these components are not simply contingent effects of anger: they are constitutive of the state. All are present in paradigm or prototypical states of anger, and they exhaust the nature of the emotion. They are conceptually linked to the concept, and not simply contingent effects of anger.

---

[25] Niedenthal (2008), p. 593.

The metaconcept that applies here is that of a cluster concept. The idea derives from Wittgenstein, especially from his often cited example of our concept of games,[26] and it has been applied more widely in recent philosophy. Berys Gaut, for example, has argued that our concept of art is of this type.[27] A cluster concept has multiple criteria for its application, none of which is necessary or sufficient. There is nothing that all games have in common, but paradigms have rules, involve competition, role playing, and so on. These criteria are conceptually linked to the application of the concept: they count necessarily toward an object's or state's being of a kind to which the concept applies, here the concept of games. Prototypical instantiations of the concept have all of the criterial cluster of properties, while less clear instantiations have some but not all of those properties. Children's games may not be competitive, and their rules may be vague, but they count as games in virtue of their imaginative role playing, although they are not prototypical games in the way that baseball is. All cluster concepts admit of paradigm as well as borderline instantiations.

The joint satisfaction of all the criterial properties is sufficient for a state's being of that kind, but so might be the instantiation of fewer than all in particular cases, although then the state will not be a paradigm of the kind. In the latter case there can be disagreement in ascribing the kind term. Is a child's momentary make-believe role a game? In some contexts we will say yes, in other contexts no. Some conditions may be necessary for the application of a cluster concept, for example in the case of emotions that they be mental states, but these conditions then define the genus and not emotions themselves. Finally, that the criterial conditions are constitutive of the state or conceptually linked to the application of the concept does not prevent these conditions from causally interacting. Explanations of some of the conditions in terms of others will be proper, for example that a person flees because he is afraid or perceives danger, even though the disposition to flee is itself part of the concept of fear. Similarly, one can tremble or sweat because of fear or feel a queasy sensation, although all of these are at the same time constituents of the emotion of fear.

[26] L. Wittgenstein (1958), pp. 31–2.   [27] B. Gaut (2000).

I have claimed that the concept of an emotion is such a cluster concept. We can now proceed to see how the concept of happiness as an emotion fits this model, and what its criterial cluster of properties is.

Happiness

Categorized as an emotion

Happiness in its primary sense is an emotion. But I noted earlier that the concept also applies in subsidiary uses to related states: attitudes and temperaments. In an attitude there is always an intentional object—one is happy about some fact or state of affairs. I am happy about the recent movement of the stock market, or that a democrat won the recent local election. As noted, such an attitude will lack the sensations, bodily symptoms, and dispositions typical of emotions. But facts about which I am happy can also make me feel happy (in the primary sense of an emotion), if I grant them a certain importance. Very good news can send a chill down my spine, make me smile, and even make me disposed to jump up and down. When we speak of a happy person, we usually refer to a person with a happy temperament, a person who is inclined to feel happy or be in a good mood often. But again we also might be referring to a person who feels happy at a time, a person in a happy emotional state.

It is the latter sense that I mainly want to capture, as I take it to be fundamental. Attitudes don't feel happy, although they can cause one to feel happy, and temperaments and moods are dispositions to feel happy. Feeling happy is an emotion, like feeling angry or fearful, or, more closely, feeling jealous or prideful. In this sense it is not true that a person is always somewhere on a happiness scale, as many philosophers and psychologists assume. There is no emotional state that people are always in, no emotion that we are always feeling to some degree. Right now I feel neither happy nor unhappy, and that is normal for me and I assume for others. I take myself to be a fairly happy person, but that does not imply that I am always feeling happy (I am not a grinning idiot). On November 9th, 2016 my temperament was still that of a happy person, but I certainly wasn't feeling happy.

When I reflect on how my life is going, or when an important goal is satisfied or frustrated, I will then often feel happy or unhappy. But that is not a constant occurrence. I am no more always somewhere on a happiness scale than I am somewhere on a fearful or jealous scale, although in a secondary use of the concept I can be a generally happy or fearful or jealous person, having a disposition to exhibit these emotions in certain triggering conditions. The contrary assumption that we are always happy or unhappy leads to faulty analyses of happiness, such as the balance of emotions over time account criticized earlier. Thus again it is not an objection to accounts that include judgments as components of happiness that we are not often judging our lives or aspects of them explicitly or implicitly. We are not often feeling particularly happy or unhappy, although we might have a happy temperament or be in a happy mood. These again are dispositional states, not constant locations on an emotional scale. Happy moods are somewhat longer-term than happy feelings or emotions, and temperaments are longer-term still.

The judgmental component

A person who is happy at a given time will prototypically be in all the components of an emotional state. We may begin with the judgmental or evaluative component that is typically central in a cognitively elaborated or higher emotion, which happiness is. This component is central because it stands at the center of the causal nexus of components, typically causing the feelings, bodily symptoms, and behavioral dispositions. As noted earlier, philosophers who make this judgment central in their analyses of happiness usually describe it as a judgment of satisfaction with one's life. But, as also noted, one can be satisfied with very bad conditions if one expected worse, and then, while a person with such a low bar might be happy (in the attitudinal sense) that conditions were not worse, she will be unlikely to be a happy person at that time or to be feeling happy. When one feels happy, one implicitly judges that one's life is going well, not simply that one is satisfied.

Robert Nozick, who is the one philosopher to characterize happiness as an emotion, including judgmental and feeling components, describes the judgment as a recognition of wanting nothing else at the time.[28] As opposed to the judgment of satisfaction, which is too weak, the judgment that one wants nothing else is too strong. I can be very happy now while still wanting to finish my next article, wanting to eat dinner, and wanting

---

[28] R. Nozick (1989), pp. 108–9.

many other things as well. As noted, better to characterize being happy at a time, feeling happy or being in the emotional state, as in part judging, usually implicitly, that one's life is going well at that time. This judgment, like a judgment of satisfaction, can be affected by how low one sets the bar, but less so than a judgment of satisfaction, since one can be satisfied without thinking that things are going well. One can also think that things are going well without being yet satisfied, if one is very ambitious and sets the bar for satisfaction very high. But that person will be reasonably happy, other things being equal (in terms of feelings), in evaluating the course of his life positively.

The primary sense of judgment in the emotion of happiness is that one's life is going well at the time of the judgment. But the time in question can extend into the past and future: reflecting on past achievements or anticipating future ones can make me happy, can lead me to judge that my life is or has been going well. For some reason philosophers have thought that the focus of the judgmental component of happiness is the subject's whole life,[29] but again judging from my own case, we very rarely reflect on our whole lives (as opposed to our lives as a whole), focusing instead, when we are reflective, on recent or anticipated segments of it. Perhaps, near the anticipated end of life, a person will be made happy or unhappy by judging how it has all gone, but even then I would suppose that one would tend to focus on its more recent segments. As noted, the judgments can differ in scope in another way as well, evaluating the way one's whole life is going or only certain major aspects of it. I can be happy in my marriage, feel happy when thinking about my marriage, or just feel happy. This is again true of other emotions as well: I can fear a particular snake, fear snakes in general (feel fearful when I think about them), be fearful of my situation generally (if I am lost in the Amazon jungle), or be a generally fearful person (temperament sense).

A controversial case regarding the evaluative component of happiness is that in which the judgment is mistaken: one thinks that one's life or some important aspect of it is going well when in fact it is not. Sam thinks that his marriage is going well, for example, when, unknown to him, his spouse has only contempt for him and is having an affair with

---

[29] Tatarkiewicz (1976) is a prime example.

someone else (note the change to the third person). Some philosophers think that authentic happiness requires correct judgments.[30] If we accept this distinction, we should be quick to point out that inauthentic happiness as an emotion is just as much happiness as the authentic variety (although not as much desired—more on that later). In this respect happiness is just like other emotions (and, of course, all the respects in which happiness is just like other emotions constitute evidence that it is itself an emotion).

I need not be correct that a spider is dangerous in order to fear it; I need not be correct that my friend has wronged me in order to be angry at him; I can be mistaken about what someone has and still be jealous of her for having it. Imagined objects can be as good as real ones in generating emotions, including happiness. Of course, when Sam finds out that he was mistaken about his wife, his marriage will no longer make him happy—he might even be more unhappy for having been mistaken. This is clearly consistent with his having been happy earlier. Likewise, when I find out that my friend has not really wronged me, I will no longer be angry at him—I might even like him better. This corrects but does not eliminate my earlier anger. Emotions most often, but not always, respond to the reasons for having them.

It is also no objection to the judgmental component of happiness that such judgments can be affected by momentary changes in moods perhaps brought about by seemingly trivial occurrences or changes in circumstances. Just as one can be angry at trivial offenses, so one's level of emotional happiness can be affected by trivial things, although one will still take oneself to be evaluating one's whole situation or major aspects of it. When the sun comes out after a storm, one can be happy that it has come out, and this can make one feel happy, improve one's emotional state. If one is not only happy about the sun's being out, but feels happy, then one implicitly judges that things are going well generally and not just in respect to the weather.

Other components

So much for the judgmental aspect of happiness. The feeling aspect is a feeling of pleasure. But again we must distinguish the proper sense

---

[30] See Haybron (2013).

of pleasure here from other related senses explained in the previous chapter. In its intentional sense, that is, taking pleasure in various things, it is once more a pro-attitude, without necessarily having any accompanying sensations. I take pleasure in the fact that the Dolphins won the game (roughly equivalent to being happy about it) without feeling any sensation when I think about it. But there are also pleasurable sensations—the pleasure of a caress or massage. As noted in the previous chapter, these are not simply sensations I take pleasure in,[31] but a distinct second sense of pleasure, since I can have pleasurable sensations that I take no pleasure in, if they are guilty or addictive pleasures, and I can take pleasure in painful sensations, if I am a masochist.[32]

The type of feeling involved in full-blown happiness is of the third kind, what I called a pure feeling. Unlike a sensation, it has no specific bodily location. Like a pro-attitude, it takes an intentional object, in this case one's life or aspects of it at a time, possibly an extended time, as noted. Unlike a pro-attitude, it is a genuine affect: it feels a certain way. Think again of the warm glow or feeling of elation you have when you learn of some major event affecting your life in a positive way, for example the acceptance of a book manuscript or marriage proposal (nice to have an author direct your attention to such feelings and their causes). Such extreme cases indicate clearly the sort of lesser but similar feelings caused by less momentous events that affect one's life favorably, all the way down to such events as the sun's coming out. This feeling is not simply a "sense of well-being," as Haybron describes what seems more akin to a judgment, but again a way of feeling, a pure affect, although taking an object and arising from an implicit judgment.

Nozick, who, as noted, also refers to happiness as an emotion, nevertheless has too narrow a view of the emotional state, limiting it to a judgment and a feeling. But the other components of prototypical emotions are present as well in full-blown happiness, making the classification perfectly apt. A person who is happy shows certain bodily symptoms: she smiles often and speaks in a cheerful tone of voice. There are behavioral tendencies as well, although they are more subtle and flexible than the fixed behavioral patterns of the basic emotions such

---

[31] Contra Feldman (2010).

[32] Feldman's analysis of masochism contains one thought too many, i.e. taking pleasure in a sensation I take displeasure in.

as fear and anger, again more like behavioral patterns associated with other cognitively rich emotions such as jealousy or pride. A happy person is more energetic and more open to new objects and explorations. According to Fredrickson and Cohn, as opposed to negative emotions that narrow options for action, "positive emotions lead to broadened and more flexible response tendencies, widening the array of thoughts and actions that come to mind." This flexibility and openness has long-term as opposed to immediate adaptive benefits.[33] A person more open to new possibilities might not benefit immediately, but he is more likely to better adapt in the long run.

Thus, happiness includes all the elements of emotions in its prototypical instances. It includes evaluative judgment, feelings of pleasure, bodily symptoms, and behavioral dispositions. We may now clarify further the central judgmental component, which will also clarify the relation of happiness to well-being, another major topic in the literature on happiness.

Happiness and Well-Being

Nonequivalence

Some philosophers simply equate welfare or well-being with happiness, or with authentic happiness, as earlier defined.[34] This equation is made more plausible by the assumption that happiness is what we ultimately or above all else want, what we wish upon our children for their future lives. What we wish for our children is what will make their lives go well for them, their welfare, and we often say that we want them only to be happy. To speak in that way is to equate happiness and well-being. But I take it to be a loose way of speaking or a confusion of a part for the whole.

I have said that happiness as an emotion centrally includes a positive evaluation of one's life or important aspects of it at a time, an implicit judgment that one's life is going well. A life that is going well is a life with a positive level of welfare or well-being. Thus happiness includes a judgment of one's welfare. But clearly this is not a judgment of one's

---

[33] Fredrickson and Cohn (2008), p. 782.
[34] Feldman (2010); Sumner (1996). See also J. W. and M. J. Mulnix (2015), pp. 191–5.

happiness, even though, like other emotions, happiness can iterate on a higher level: it is possible to be happy that one is happy (especially if one has been recently unhappy).

On my view happiness and welfare are distinct but closely related in several ways. For one thing, well-being is not an emotion, but again the object of the judgmental component of the emotion of happiness. This distinction emerges most clearly when that judgment is mistaken, as in the case of the deceived spouse described earlier. The life of this unfortunate dupe is not going well, although he mistakenly thinks it is and is therefore happy. Likewise with a terminally ill person who thinks she is healthy. Happiness and well-being come apart in all such cases. Happiness can result from wishful thinking or delusion, from trivial pursuits or from drugs. Well-being is more anchored to reality.

Preview of well-being

I will defend a view of well-being at length in the next chapter. Here I will indicate only enough of the view to make clear its relations to happiness. According to this view, well-being consists in the satisfaction of one's central rational desires. Desires are rational if coherent (the satisfaction of some does not prevent the satisfaction of others more central) and relevantly informed (mainly informed of what it is like to satisfy them). Desires are central when connected to many others and deemed important by the subject. A person whose deepest desires are being satisfied has a good life, a life that is going well for him, although he might not be a good person, and his life might not be judged to be good by others whose values are different. The very rich hedge fund manager who cares most about money is leading a good life for him, no matter how much academic philosophers might condemn his way of life and deny its value (with the claim that their values are objective).

What is central or important to a subject will shift with time, so that my most important thing to do or desire to fulfill now might be to walk my dog or take a rest. And seemingly trivial desires can be linked to more central ones, making them not trivial at the time. My desire for a good meal can contribute to the fulfillment of my standing desire to have some pleasant sensations and relaxing times. Thus some seemingly trivial things can add to one's welfare, while pursuing mere whims will not. That the satisfaction of relevantly uninformed desires does not add to welfare when one is mistaken about what it is like to satisfy them is compatible with the recognition that mistaken judgments of welfare can be components of happiness: they are still (mistaken) judgments that rational or relevantly informed desires are being satisfied. Since happiness has physical symptoms and includes behavioral dispositions that are sometimes manifested, it is generally easier to judge whether another person is happy than it is to judge her level of welfare. But if we have a good idea of what she desires and achieves, then it becomes easier to judge her welfare.

This account will avoid objections to other desire satisfaction accounts of personal welfare by excluding desires whose satisfaction does not contribute to welfare: shallow or trivial desires at a time (not central); those whose satisfaction disappoints (not informed); and self-destructive or self-defeating desires (not coherent). Other more controversial examples are also handled. Does my desire that the war in Syria end contribute to my welfare if satisfied? It depends on how central that desire is for me, how many other desires of mine it connects to or generates, and how important to my life I deem it to be. What about pleasant surprises not desired in advance, or things such as kale that are good for me although not desired? The latter add to my welfare because connected to other things I desire, such as good health. The former, pleasant surprises, might so connect as well, and would be desired with information of what it is like to satisfy desires for them.

The main alternatives to such an account of welfare are objective list, hedonist, and perfectionist accounts. Objective lists claim objectivity while reflecting what their authors take to be good for people or to contribute to their flourishing as humans. As for perfectionism, the development or full realization of social, intellectual, and physical capacities is one life project, albeit a rather egocentric one, that can organize many activities and more specific desires, but there are many other central concerns that can play the same role without being so focused on oneself. My son has artistic talent that he has not developed, but I do not take this to detract from his welfare.

In regard to objective lists not restricted to developing human capacities, they will of course vary with the author. Among philosophers, intellectual achievements are likely to be high on the list, but being in tune with nature will not be mentioned, while the farmer's list is likely to be the reverse. There are admittedly some things virtually all people want or need: food, shelter, perhaps some personal relationships . . . But that list is quite small and certainly does not exhaust the good life for people. Beyond those things, desires or tastes vary without limit, and, as is commonly objected, if the proposed goods connect with none of a subject's desires, with nothing she cares about or is concerned with, it is very hard to see how their provision would make her life go better.

Relation of happiness to well-being

If we start with the premise that happiness is our most important value, what we want most in life, then we will infer some kind of desire satisfaction or human flourishing account of happiness. Then we will also equate happiness with well-being. But we have seen that this equation is wrong. What we want most, and most obviously, for ourselves and our children is well-being. In fact, if well-being is as I have defined it, it is tautologous that we desire well-being, since to (rationally) desire is to desire to have the desire satisfied (meta-desires, like meta-emotions, should not be puzzling). It is also more important to us that we have well-being, that our central rational desires are satisfied, than that we judge that they are satisfied, even given the pleasant feelings that come with such judgments. But since we also desire happiness, to have this pleasant emotion and be disposed to have it, happiness will be part of well-being, although certainly not the whole of it. Since happiness is part, but only part, of well-being, it cannot match its importance.

As just noted, we do desire happiness, all aspects of it, although not as centrally as we desire well-being. We desire not only to have our most important desires satisfied, but also to know or judge correctly that they are being satisfied. We want not only good lives for our children, but for them to be satisfied with their lives or judge that they are good. And we desire not only the very pleasant feeling that accompanies this knowledge, but also the effects on our outlooks and resulting behavioral dispositions: we want to be optimistic and therefore energetic and open to new possibilities and opportunities. Furthermore, since we generally know when our desires are being satisfied, our judgments of well-being that are central to happiness are generally correct. The status of our important desires generally determines our judgments of whether our lives are going well or badly. Therefore, happiness not only reflects well-being, but is extensionally equivalent to its more transparent and higher levels, which explains why it is proverbially claimed that happiness is our highest good or what we most desire. Happiness tracks welfare and is therefore easily confused with it (more easily confused under hedonistic theories of both welfare and happiness).

What about the recognition that people sometimes appear willing to sacrifice their happiness for other goods? Is this a problem for an account that sees happiness and well-being to be so closely related in the ways I have described? The usual case is that of someone trying to achieve a very difficult goal, trying to fulfill some desire deemed most important that requires sacrificing other goods in the meantime. If that goal is never achieved, the person will indeed have sacrificed both well-being and happiness (assuming that its pursuit is not in itself most rewarding, since otherwise the person would not be sacrificing either). If the goal is achieved, then greater happiness should ensue along with the boost in welfare. What the person was willing to do therefore was to forego some interim well-being and happiness for the prospect of a higher level of both later, sacrifice the satisfaction of some desires for the possibility of satisfying more central ones. Whether that risk is rational depends on the odds of success and the importance of the goal or boost in welfare its achievement would provide. But in any case, the example does not show that welfare and happiness come apart in any way problematic for my account of their relations.

A more drastic if more farfetched example is our refusal to enter Nozick's pleasure or happiness virtual reality machine, which guarantees a life of bliss, albeit not one connected to the real world. It appears in the machine that all our desires are being satisfied, and so we judge it to be so and are happy. But given our present desires for real relationships and achievements, we do not now judge that we would have well-being in the machine. Thus our refusal to enter shows only that we value genuine well-being, the satisfaction of central desires we presently have, over happiness, and I have been arguing for that priority. For the same reason we would not simply exchange our present desires for others more easily satisfied, even if we could.

To summarize, as an emotion happiness includes a judgment of a positive level of well-being and is at the same time itself part of well-being in being centrally desired by virtually all people (only extreme guilt feelings might cancel that desire). Well-being causes happiness as well as including it, and once more the causal relations run in both directions. My being happy contributes to my well-being since I rationally desire to be happy, and the satisfaction of the desires that constitute well-being makes me happy. Happiness results from achieving my goals, but also makes it easier to achieve them. As noted earlier, a happy person tends to be more energetic and adaptable. While I am always at some level of welfare in that certain of my desires are being satisfied and others frustrated or delayed, the emotion of happiness, like other emotions, is intermittent and temporary, although I can be disposed to be happy or not, be a happy person or not.

We may now conclude by reiterating and further clarifying the relation of happiness to other emotions, showing further why happiness in its primary sense is itself best classified as an emotion.

Relation to Other Emotions

Parallels

I have argued that full-blown happiness has all the components of proto-typical emotions: cognitive, that is, evaluative judgment or appraisal; affective, a pure feeling without specific bodily location but with an intentional object; physical, symptoms such as smiling; and behavioral dispositional, tending to be energetic and open to new explorations. There are parallels to other emotions as well. First, there is, of course, the language we use: "I feel angry," "I feel afraid," "I am jealous," "I feel happy," "I am happy." Such locutions apply to all emotions, happiness included. They indicate that these states have both judgmental and affective elements.

Second, as noted, the judgmental component in happiness need not be correct in order to produce the other components of the emotion, and this is the same with other emotions. Just as I need not be correct that my life is going well in order for that judgment to make me happy, so I need not be correct that a snake is dangerous in order to fear it. Sam need not be correct that his spouse is faithful in order for his marriage to make him happy, and I can be angry at someone who has not really wronged me.

Third, happiness can iterate in the same way as other emotions. I can be happy that I feel happy, having just finished my third glass of wine. In the same way I can fear that I will be fearful when having to do something that takes courage. When I used to have to play trumpet solos, I was always afraid that I would fear missing a high note, and therefore would miss it. Fourth, happiness, like other emotions, comes in occurrent and dispositional forms (the latter being moods or temperaments). I can feel happy at a time or be a happy person, just as I can feel pride or be a prideful person. A happy person is disposed to feel happy, to smile, and to go about her work efficiently. A prideful person is disposed to feel pride, puff out his chest, and boast of his achievements.

There are other more subtle similarities as well. A much discussed phenomenon relating to happiness is adaptation. Positive events, achievements, or acquisitions can dramatically raise the level of happiness in the short term, can make one feel the emotion intensely or be disposed to feel it short term when thinking of those things. But in the longer run people tend to return to their prior levels or dispositions, so that the best predictor of how happy a person will be at the end of any time sequence is how happy she was (how she judged her life to be going) at the beginning.[35] This makes another parallel to other emotions because in general repeated exposure to emotion-causing stimuli over time will tend to reduce their effects. A main treatment for phobias, for example, is repeated exposure to the feared triggers. Thus adaptation in the case of happiness may be just an instance of a more general emotional phenomenon. Adaptation is adaptive in the evolutionary sense: remaining on a blissful hedonic level could hinder other achievements or sober reactions to changes in the environment. Similarly for other intense emotions. Fear is adaptive in prompting swift flights from danger, but being in a constant state of fear blocks other useful actions.

Another relevant phenomenon is the so-called paradox of happiness. The more we strive self-consciously to be happy, the less happy we tend to be. We tend to be most happy when in the flow and not thinking about trying to be happy. But again this is true of other emotions as well. If I face an important and daunting challenge and simply tell myself not to be afraid, simply dwell on it and try not to feel fear (as opposed to seeking therapy), I am likely to be more fearful. If I tell myself not to be prideful

---

[35] D. Nettle (2005), p. 92. It might be thought that the phenomenon of adaptation poses a problem for a desire satisfaction theory of well-being such as I have proposed, since it seems to show that satisfaction of even rational desires does not raise the level of personal welfare long term. Two responses can be made. First, the satisfaction of a central rational desire does have an immediate positive effect on well-being. Second, the level of well-being measures overall satisfaction of rational desires, and since, when some are satisfied, others will arise and take their central place, the overall level will tend to remain relatively stable.

or jealous, I am likely to be more so. This is compatible with the possibility that we can train ourselves through indirect means not to be so prideful or jealous. I remain neutral about whether there also could be books that might train us to be happier. But just wishing or intending not to fear or feel jealous is not more efficacious than just aiming to be happy. Once again happiness is no different in this regard from other emotions, although philosophers have much remarked on the phenomenon only in its case.

Borderline cases

Finally, both happiness and other emotions admit of similar borderline cases when some of the components of prototypical emotional states are missing. Since Kendall Walton's seminal work on fiction,[36] there has been a lively debate about whether emotional reactions to fictional narratives are genuine. Such states involve the ordinary sensations, so that they feel the same as other emotions, but they involve imaginings instead of beliefs or judgments and lack the usual behavioral dispositions. When, prompted by the screen, I imagine that the movie monster is approaching but do not believe he really is and am not inclined to flee the theater, do I then really feel fear? When I feel the symptoms of anger at Iago's malicious machinations but am not inclined to rush the stage and throttle him, am I truly angry? Walton says no, I only imagine or make-believe that I feel genuine fear or anger. Others, including myself, have argued yes, since emotions that are less than prototypical in lacking some of the criterial components can still be genuine emotions, albeit not paradigms. I feel fear watching the horror movie and anger at Iago, but these are not the full-blown or prototypical instances of these emotions. I say the same about certain borderline instances of happiness.

Recall two opposed characters: one who is cheerful while not judging that her life is going well, and one who judges his life to be going well and yet feels down. Feldman's variation on the first takes a drug that makes her feel better while recognizing that her central desire to finish her dissertation has no greater chance of success. Feldman claims that she is happier even though her judgment of the status of her unfulfilled

---

[36] K. Walton (1990).

desires has not changed.[37] It is more plausible that she recognizes an improvement in the status of one central desire, the desire that she not have such negative feelings. And her better mood probably allows her to focus less on her unfinished dissertation and more on desires she is able to satisfy. A more plausible character who has taken the drug might even be more optimistic about finishing her dissertation. In any case, we would hesitate to call her a fully happy person unless she feels the desire to finish her dissertation much less urgently or grants it much less importance. Then she would judge her well-being, the status of her desires, differently. Thus Feldman is right that she is happier after the drug but wrong that her judgments of her level of desire satisfaction have not changed. Even so, given the status of her central desire to finish her dissertation, she is a borderline case.

The same hesitation is true of our appraisal of the second character. He is happy with his job and marriage—central concerns—but he is not fully happy in having negative feelings (and presumably the desire not to have them). Some of his central desires are being satisfied, but an important one, not to feel constantly down, is not. So his judgment of well-being should be affected, not being wholly positive or negative. Again he is a borderline case. Thus happiness, like other emotions such as fear (in the case of fearing fictions), admits of the same kind of borderline cases when some but not all of the components of the prototypical instances are present.

Summary

I conclude that happiness is certainly an emotion, with the same characteristics as other emotions, the same structural makeup and causal nexus as other states always classified as emotions. It is a cognitively elaborated positive emotional state involving a judgment of how one's life is going, physical symptoms, feelings, and having more subtle and longer-term rather than immediate and fixed behavioral effects—a state similar to jealousy or pride. Recognizing happiness as primarily an emotion, with subsidiary senses as an attitude, mood, or temperament, allows us to see what the previously dominant views, which focused

---

[37] F. Feldman (2010), pp. 64–6.

on some components of the state but not others, got right and what they got wrong.

The account of happiness as an emotion incorporates all of what they got right. It also places the value of happiness and its place in our motivations in proper perspective. Its exaggerated place in the history of philosophy and more recent psychology, intended to guide social policy, stems from its confusion with well-being, to which we now turn in detail.

Well-Being

Criteria for Theory Choice

The main candidate accounts of well-being in the philosophical literature are hedonism, perfectionism, broader objective list accounts, a more recent causal network account, and desire satisfaction accounts. I will evaluate these alternatives according to the usual criteria for theory choice. First, an acceptable theory must capture the relevant data. In this case it must capture our established concept of personal welfare or well-being instead of changing the subject. Our account must state necessary and sufficient conditions for a person to have a good life, a life that is going well. Contributors to well-being are those things that benefit a person, that are good for her, that have prudential value for her.[1] Well-being is what makes life valuable or good for the individual whose life it is. This definition is not controversial[2] and must be captured by any acceptable theory of well-being. It will be captured if it implies our settled judgments of what is good for individual persons, what makes their lives go well.

Second, a good theory should unify and explain the data. In this case it should explain why the various things that make a person's life go well do so. It should, if possible, unify the various sources of well-being under a common concept. Preferably it should show what those things, if they are numerous on a common sense level, have in common. Third, and related

---

[1] Compare Campbell (2016), p. 403.

[2] See, for example, Moore (2000). Another well-known definition of personal welfare is that of Stephen Darwall (2002). For him a person's welfare consists in what we ought to desire for her in so far as we care for her. In my view this definition fails because it allows our judgment to be clouded by our own values, which would then be wrongly substituted for the subject's values. This is not a problem from Darwall's point of view, since he believes in and appeals here to objective values that we ought to desire for the person we care for. But I argue here and elsewhere against the concept of objective values.

to the second criterion, a good account of well-being should show why we are primarily motivated to pursue and achieve it for ourselves and for others, if we care about them. It should demonstrate the normative force of well-being, why we aim at it, and rationally should aim at it. An account that leaves it puzzling why we are motivated to pursue our own welfare cannot be acceptable, since it is a given that we are so motivated.

This is not to say that we aim at well-being de dicto, that is, self-consciously or conceived as such. There is a paradox of well-being similar to the paradoxes of pleasure and happiness (predictably, since they are typically parts of well-being). If we aim at any of these directly, we are less likely to achieve them. Like pleasure and happiness, well-being is in an extended sense a byproduct of getting what we rationally desire. Not literally a byproduct, since on the account I will defend, well-being simply *is* (knowingly) getting what we rationally desire. Since it consists in satisfying other desires, it disappears from view when we try to aim directly at it, which is why we are likely to be frustrated when we try simply to lead the good life. But in pursuing our rational aims, we are pursuing the good life for us. My account will therefore maintain the tightest link between well-being and our motivation to pursue it. But it is a criterion of any acceptable account of well-being that it explains this motivation.

Other Accounts

Hedonism

With these criteria in mind I will spend the bulk of this chapter defending a rational desire satisfaction account of well-being, one that avoids the standard objections to previous versions. Prior to that defense, and given reasonable limitations of space, I will state or review what I take to be fatal objections to the alternative accounts. We may begin with the most easily refuted view, one that we have already dismissed by implication in previous chapters: hedonism. Hedonists generally equate well-being with happiness, and then with a balance of pleasure account of happiness. In favor of this account is the fact that it can explain our motivation to pursue well-being, since we are generally motivated to pursue pleasure. It also offers a unifying explanation for our pursuit of diverse other things that appear to be good for us. Different people find pleasure in different objects and activities, but hedonists claim that what matters for well-being is that all these pursuits, when successful, produce pleasure in the end. I like tennis and my neighbor likes picnics; for the hedonist what these activities have in common is that we find pleasure in them.

I have argued, however, that the balance of pleasure account is too narrow to capture even our concept of happiness, which includes as well a judgment that one's life is going well. Furthermore, happiness is only one component of well-being. Remember that well-being is the all-inclusive category of personal value, of what makes a person's life go well for him or her. Although we do sometimes aim at pleasure, especially in food and sex, such things as achievements, knowledge, and relationships, beyond the feelings of pleasure or happiness they produce, are also valued and valuable for individuals. Remember also that well-being is what we inclusively aim at. In regard to sensory pleasure, unless you are Don Giovanni or Falstaff, such pleasures will be only a relatively small source of motivation. (If you think that I am a pathetic ascetic intellectual for dismissing the life of Don Juan so quickly, and that most men at least would gladly opt for such a life, I would reply that unless you look and could act like the Don, an attempt to imitate him would result in a life of constant frustration, not sexual conquest, as most of us know from our younger days.)

On a similar note, Nozick's pleasure machine, described in the previous chapter, illustrated how many other things we aim at besides sensual pleasure. For those of us who would refuse to enter, it refutes as well the intentional or attitudinal kind of pleasure, taking pleasure in various things, as exhaustive of well-being, since the machine can provide endless sources of intentional pleasure. This second and more frequent kind of pleasure was also seen to be a byproduct of fulfilling our aims (as is the third pure feeling kind of pleasure),[3] not their primary target. This argument against the hedonist account of well-being will not work for those who would willingly enter the pleasure machine even for life, as some of my students indicated they would. What their response indicates to me, if they are sincere and reflective, is that they care more for pleasure

---

[3] Return to the first chapter, Pleasure, "The Nature and Types of Pleasure," to be reminded of these distinctions.

than for authentic achievements and relationships, indeed care more for pleasure than for any genuine contact with the real world. But if this priority among desires or concerns explains their preference for the pleasure machine, and if this preference connotes the primary source of their well-being, this suggests a desire satisfaction account of well-being instead of a hedonist account. And the response of the majority still blocks the latter. Most prefer not to enter, as Nozick assumed, once they reflect on how much would be lost.

The degree to which sensory pleasures contribute to the well-being of different individuals seems to depend on how much they desire or care about such pleasures. I find warm baths mildly pleasurable but do not desire them enough to take the trouble to indulge. I prefer the ease of a shower or the pleasure of a massage. Others might have the opposite preferences. And people vary as well in how much they care about sensory pleasures generally, as opposed to, say, achievements and relationships. How much such pleasures contribute to their well-being in turn seems to depend on how much they care about them.

As for taking pleasure in various things, this is not only normally a byproduct and not a source of motivation, but it is questionable whether some instances contribute to well-being at all. Does taking pleasure in unworthy objects—pornography, very bad art or music, or the suffering of others—contribute to well-being? Hedonists might offer discounts to such contribution in these cases, but then they are moving toward objective list accounts. The account I will defend would judge such cases in terms of whether desires for such objects fit into informed and coherent motivational sets. Does pleasure taken in bad art, for example, block deeper satisfactions that could be derived from improved taste in better art? Is such improvement possible and worth the trouble in terms of the individual's other aims and capacities, etc.?

Hedonists can allow that pleasures that block the acquisition of greater pleasures do not contribute net positively to well-being. But just as it is clear that we desire other things, so it is equally clear that the satisfaction of these desires—for knowledge, achievement, relationships, and so on—contributes to well-being. My desire to finish writing this book is independent of whether I think doing so will maximize pleasure, as opposed to other things I could be doing. But I take it that its satisfaction will maximize my well-being, as opposed to other things I could do.

Objective lists

If it is clear that things other than pleasure can contribute to well-being, we can move on to broader objective list accounts. According to such accounts, what is good for us is independent of our desires or concerns, our subjective states. Vegetables are good for children whatever their desires or lack of them. Children in general lend support to this theory of prudential goods since they appear to have few developed rational desires and yet many things are good for them, as their parents point out to them without much effect on their motivations. Some things seem objectively good or bad for adults too. Banging one's head against the wall or failing to save for old age seem bad whatever one's current desires. The student who desires to party and not study is not serving her welfare by following her seemingly strongest desire at the time. So these accounts list multiple goods independent of desires or other pro-attitudes as constituents of well-being. According to them, hedonism is one such account with an implausibly short list (although not if intentional pleasure (pro-attitude) is intended).

A typical list of objective prudential goods is provided by James Griffin. It includes accomplishment, autonomy and liberty, minimum material goods, understanding or knowledge, enjoyment, and deep personal relationships.[4] To these might have been added health, security, happiness, and development of natural capacities . . . Such lists capture at least some of our intuitive judgments about what contributes to our welfare. They improve on hedonism by including other goods that we recognize as such. They avoid some of the problems that seem to afflict desire satisfaction accounts, such as desiring bad things or not desiring good things (to be solved in a later section).

One problem here, if we simply provide the objective list, is that the account fails to satisfy our criteria for a good theory. There is no unifying explanation for the various items on the list. The only thing that unites them is that they are supposed to be good. If this goodness that is supposed to unite them is objective, independent of subjective attitudes or desires, there is introduced a mysterious non-natural property of value, with no explanation for what has this property and how we are supposed to know what has it, save for an equally mysterious intuition.

---

[4] Griffin (1986), p. 67.

By contrast, if we seek a natural unifying property, it seems that what makes it on the list is simply what most people deeply desire. As John Stuart Mill pointed out, the only way we know that something is desirable is that people desire it.

Furthermore, with no unifying explanation for why just those items appear on any given objective list, it seems that what we have is at best a (partial) list of sources or contributors to well-being (of most people) without any insight as to what well-being is. In like manner, good nutrition and exercise contribute to good health, but they do not constitute or explain what good health is. We want first to know what well-being is before we can reliably judge whether some item belongs on a list of its sources. Even a complete list of its sources would not seem to reveal its nature, tell us what it is in the most basic sense. Simply appealing to intuition to confirm the items on a list is making this appeal one step too early, in Rawlsian terms settling for narrow rather than wide reflective equilibrium. And one again suspects that the list will reflect only the intuitions or concerns of its author, especially given that the lists of different authors will differ.

A second problem just indicated, and suggested by my noting what might have been added to Griffin's list, is that any such list will be partial and provincial, reflective of its author's central concerns and priorities. Writing in pre-terrorist times, Griffin did not include security on his list, a central, indeed obsessive or paranoid, concern of many current voters. Most people in our present society seem to think that a life without security from physical harm cannot be a good life, even if such harm never materializes. The Nebraskans who think that Isis is coming to get them would not share Griffin's priorities. Nor would many others. As an academic, he rates accomplishment and knowledge highly, but there is no mention of being in tune with nature or appreciating natural beauty. A farmer's, gardener's, or environmentalist's list might well reflect the opposite priority. And what are we to say of people who don't care much about certain items on the list, or who might even find them abhorrent?

Griffin includes deep personal relationships. Of course this is not simply an idiosyncratic preference on his part; we are, it seems, naturally social animals who often need each other's support. But this does not prevent there being anti-social loners (less pejoratively, those who prefer solitude) for whom what to others is a deep and satisfying personal relationship would be a painful invasion of privacy. The objectivist will respond that even such a person would be better off if he were more gregarious and open. But the question is whether a naturally shy person who cannot and does not want to be gregarious would be better off if somehow forced to be in a close relationship.[5] Would that automatically add to her welfare? Even for normally social people, too many close personal relationships might make their lives too complicated, and what makes too many will again vary with temperament and motivation.

The personal value of some of the other items on Griffin's list also seems to depend on whether they are desired by particular individuals. Does more knowledge or understanding always make a person better off? Aside from understanding or knowing things that are very detrimental to one's happiness, there is boundless useless knowledge that is entirely irrelevant to welfare. Knowing how many stones are in my driveway or how many blades of grass are in my lawn would not add to my welfare in any way. Knowledge that does benefit me is knowledge I desire to have or knowledge that facilitates the satisfaction of my other desires. Once again, an item on the list adds to my well-being if and seemingly only if it fits my motivational set or contributes to the satisfaction of my rational desires.

Will any such list, no matter how expanded with desire-independent goods, suffice to capture well-being? Can any person score a perfect ten for well-being by having everything on some objective list but still not be getting what she most wants and feeling constantly frustrated by not having it? Can any list hope to exhaust what every individual most deeply desires, and, if not, will it capture even the sources of welfare for each person? Any such list will reflect the central desires of its author or, at best, of most people. Can an item make it on a list if no one cares about it even with full knowledge of its nature and relations to other desires? The semi-rhetorical nature of these questions indicates the collapse of any plausible list into a desire satisfaction account of well-being.

I will return to the issue of very diverse concerns below. Simply pointing out initially that different individuals have very different desires and concerns raises a third problem of the relation of well-being as characterized on objective lists to motivation. Remember that the final criterion for an acceptable theory of well-being is that it show why we

---

[5] Compare Tiberius (2015), p. 159.

are, ought to be, and indeed must be, if we are rational, motivated to aim at it for ourselves and for those we care about. As many philosophers agree, a subject cannot be completely alienated from her own well-being. There cannot be an intelligible demand that all her central concerns be other than they are (unless, perhaps, she is a fully programmed robot). If, say, at a certain age a person cares nothing for (further) accomplishments and wants only a life of relaxation and ease, can the author of a list like Griffin's demand that he continue to be motivated to pursue accomplishments (once I finish this book, I hope not)?

The whole idea of an objective list is that it designate personal goods or contributors to welfare that are independent of people's desires or motivations. But we have recognized that personal welfare, as the all-inclusive category of goods for individual persons, is what each of us aims at in whole. The objectivist will have a hard time, to say the least, explaining how a person is supposed to be motivated to pursue some item on his list that the individual cares nothing about. The objectivist cannot satisfy the requirement for motivation by saying that the item, if not directly desired, must at least connect with others of the person's central desires. If it doesn't, then the demand will be empty; if it does, then its appearance on the list is again justified by its connection to existing desires, a subjective criterion.

I return then to the claim that what explains the appearance of items on any list is what its author takes most people to desire, most often reflecting her own desires. That strongly suggests the collapse of the objective list account into a satisfaction of desire account of well-being. The latter seems to be the more fundamental notion of what personal welfare is. Yet another problem for the objectivist who admits this ground for including items on his list (perhaps the hybrid theorist, which Griffin appears to be, who requires that items on his list be both rationally desired and objectively good) is the appeal to most or normal people. What of the welfare of people who are not so normal or usual in their central concerns? How large a group must share a desire in order for its object to qualify as a normal, let alone objective, contributor to well-being? Any answer seems arbitrary.

Some items on objective lists refer to basic needs. Some are necessary for survival, for example minimal material goods; others are desired to some degree by virtually all people, for example knowledge and enjoyment. Some objective lists are meant to indicate the proper objects of our moral concerns, or intended to guide government policy decisions regarding what must be guaranteed to citizens. Restriction to basic needs or near universal concerns then makes sense. The state cannot be concerned to satisfy citizens' desires beyond those. But the satisfaction of basic needs certainly does not exhaust well-being, and beyond that satisfaction what contributes to personal welfare varies radically not only from culture to culture, but from individual to individual.

Tibetan monks, Hollywood celebrities, and investment bankers have very different conceptions of their personal welfare. A new tennis racquet contributes to my welfare only because of my desire to play better tennis. A new guitar would benefit my neighbor but not me. The objectivist must admit such individual differences, but she will seek to reduce them to a single item on her list, for example the enjoyment or pleasure to be derived from such objects. The objectivist becomes a partial hedonist, while the hedonist captures only a part of the objectivist's list. The reduction once again fails for a now familiar reason: I desire and there-fore aim not at the pleasure from playing better tennis, but simply at playing better tennis. If I desire this kind of achievement, then playing better tennis contributes to my welfare whether or not I get pleasant sensations or warm glows from reflecting on my victories afterward.

Pluralism among values should suggest not a substantive unifying reduction to one item on an objective list, but a formal non-substantive unifying account of what well-being is. Again, what unites all the diverse goods that contribute to different individuals' personal welfare is not that they all produce pleasure (of any of the three kinds), but that they are all rationally desired. The objectivist will say that they are desired because valuable; the subjectivist maintains the converse. But then again only the latter avoids appeal to an elusive non-natural property that mysteriously unites all these natural objects while not being perceivable in any ordin-ary way. The subjectivist or desire satisfaction theorist has the simpler explanation, leaving fewer (or no) unanswerable questions.

A final problem for the objectivist, related to the last point, is the problem of measurement. If the items on his list cannot be reduced to a single common denominator, how are they to be measured against one another to calculate overall well-being when they conflict in particular contexts? Individuals will have different priorities and preferences, but these will reflect the strengths or priorities among their desires, not objective value, which would be the same for all. How much liberty should be sacrificed for security, how much enjoyment for knowledge, and so on? Desire satisfaction theories can provide answers, but they will take into account differences in individual priorities. Appeals to objective value will fail to reflect these differences and therefore will fail to measure the well-being of different individuals. Answers limited to such appeals will again appear arbitrary, or, more likely, they will be nonexistent. A last gasp recourse might be appeal to the objective value of desire satisfaction, but clearly that would be superfluous in the present context.

Perfectionism

I can be somewhat briefer in critically commenting on another relative of objective list accounts, a briefer objective list with a different rationale— perfectionism. This account begins from a broader notion of what is good for various things, including especially living things. What is good for various things is what allows them to fulfill their functions or maximally realize their natures or capabilities. What is good for cars are such things as oil and gas; what is good for plants, sunlight and water, is what allows them to flourish as plants. Likewise, what is good for humans is what allows them to fulfill their natures. They fulfill their human nature, they flourish as humans, when they fully develop their human capacities: mental or rational, physical, and social. In this way they perfect themselves as humans by realizing their distinctively human abilities.

Such accounts have one major advantage over other objective list accounts: they do provide a unifying explanation for why items are on the list. Items belong there when they constitute or result from essentially human capacities. Thus knowledge can be taken to result from the development of our rational capacities, close personal relationships from the development of our social natures, accomplishments from physical and rational development. The first problem, however, is that development of capacities necessary for knowledge, friendship, and achievement seems valuable mainly as means to these things that are valuable in themselves. Well-being seems to consist in having the things that are intrinsically valuable, not in developing the means to get them. In further support of this claim is that few of us maximally develop our capacities just for the sake of doing so. We develop them to the extent necessary to achieve other ends or objects that we might desire.

The second problem is that not every item on a typical objective list such as that provided above will be captured. Where does pleasure, happiness, or meaning fit in, or minimal material goods? A nice rest in a hammock right now might contribute to my welfare, but one would be very hard pressed to explain how it relates to my developed capacities (for sleep?) The perfectionist might reply that only capacities that can be developed should be, and a capacity for sleep will not qualify. But getting enough sleep contributes to my welfare even if it does not represent a developed capacity. Then too, a person who has developed her capacities to the fullest but is still miserable and strongly desiring things she does not have will not seem to have a high level of well-being.

Other disqualifying problems derive first from the appeal to human nature, which is a somewhat vague and questionable notion in itself. Allowing that it can be properly regimented, the concept will surely include capacities that we would not want on a general list of personal goods: capacities for cruelty and deceptiveness, for example, that are distinctively human. Thus, not only are there too few goods included in the perfectionist's list; there are also too many. The general problem is deciding which capacities are to be included. Not those that are unique to humans, for there may be other rational or social creatures (bees and ants are arguably more social, and my dog Charlie certainly is). And almost all animals are superior in some respect to humans physically: stronger, faster, capable of flight, etc.

Either we again rely only on intuitions of which capacities are good to develop, or we include those that we desire to have developed. Relying on intuitions regarding which capacities are good to develop, which benefit us or contribute to our well-being, is circular and seemingly cannot be used to define well-being. The perfectionist can reply that this method is simply an instance of reflective equilibrium and not viciously circular. But then perfectionism loses whatever advantage it had over objective list theories in explanatory force. It no longer explains why items are on the list in a non-question-begging way. If instead the perfectionist appeals to those capacities we rationally desire to have developed, his account collapses into desire satisfaction at the deepest level. In neither case is the fundamental intuition related simply to the development of distinctly human capacities.

This problem can be avoided by dropping the appeal to human nature and speaking only of each individual's developing her capacities. But first, we once again will not want to refer to all of a person's capacities, but only those that it is desirable to develop. Second, and perhaps more damaging, developing one's capacities to the fullest seems neither necessary nor sufficient for well-being. I do not feel that I am sacrificing welfare by not lifting more weights and further developing my physical capacities. Presently facing hip surgery for a second time, I am in fact wondering whether I would have been better off if I had ignored more of my athletic potential, such as it was and is. My son showed real artistic talent when young but decided not to develop it (or simply neglected it), for which decision I don't see him as significantly worse off. He has plenty of things to do that he cares more about. More generally, children who have not yet developed their natural capacities would automatically rank low in welfare according to this account, despite being perfectly normal, well cared for, and happy. Thus developing natural capacities does not seem necessary for well-being. Even the best off among us will have many undeveloped potentials that we are simply not interested in pursuing. Would the perfectionist force us to do so?

A variant on the individual capacity account is Dan Haybron's account of well-being as individual nature fulfillment.[6] He sees well-being as fulfilling one's emotional nature so as to be happy. This is almost equivalent to satisfying one's rational desires (my account), since doing so makes one feel happy far more often than not. Haybron argues by example that the two accounts can come apart in relation to a character who would be happy owning a model train store, but who becomes a farmer because he thinks it more worthwhile and desires to do what is worthwhile.

I raise three questions in response: (1) Would this person really be happier in the store if he places great importance on doing something worthwhile? (2) How important is feeling happy to well-being in someone who judges that what he is doing is not worthwhile? (3) If one desires to sacrifice narrow self-interest to broad (in my sense), can't he be better off for doing so, that is, isn't the virtuous life better for at least some people? The upshot of these three questions is to raise doubt as to whether Haybron's character would be happy in either the train store or on the farm. The character is in the unenviable position of conflict in

---

[6] Haybron (2013).

the criteria for happiness—his judgment of his life does not align with his feelings. Haybron has him happy in the train store, but he will not be if his present desire to do with his life what is worthwhile by his own lights and his judgment of the worthlessness of running a store remain the same.

In regard to sufficiency, it seems that on the usual perfectionist account we must regard Bill Bradley, Jack Kemp, and Byron White as the best off individuals, those who must score ten for well-being, since they achieved the highest levels of sports (physical capacities) and government (rational and social capacities (not?)). They were all super professional athletes as well as being a congressman, senator, and Supreme Court justice. Yet if any of them remained always depressed and frustrated for not having been President, we would rate them significantly lower on the scale of personal well-being. For all we know, any of them might not have had such a good life despite developing these diverse capacities to the fullest. Yet compared to them, all of us would be ranked very much lower in well-being by the perfectionist.

We enjoy not so much developing our capacities as we enjoy exercising them. We take pleasure in exercising our mental capacities in appreciating works of art[7] and in intellectual endeavors. We enjoy exercising our physical capacities in sports and manual labor. And we find pleasure in socializing with others. These sources of enjoyment in the exercise of our capacities lends plausibility to the perfectionist account of well-being. But the exercise of these rational, physical, and social capacities is not quite the same as their development which, by contrast, can be painstaking. And once more it is the effects made possible by their development as means that seem intrinsically valuable. We are motivated to develop ourselves in order to be able to obtain what we desire, whereas, as emphasized earlier, we do not need to ask why we are motivated to satisfy our desires since desiring is being so motivated.

Other accounts: causal networks

I will little more than critically mention a final more recent alternative account, the causal network theory. Michael Bishop's account is intended to capture the subject matter of positive psychology.[8] This relatively

---

[7] For an account of aesthetic value along these lines, see Goldman (1995).

[8] Bishop (2015), p. 60.

recent branch of psychology studies positive causal networks and their fragments, consisting of emotions (e.g. happiness), attitudes (e.g. optimism), traits (e.g. friendliness), and accomplishments (e.g. career success, relationships). These fragments causally interact in networks so as to reinforce one another. A happy, optimistic, and friendly person will have more career success, and career success in turn might well make the person happier and more optimistic. This interaction sustains the network and can make it progressively stronger, making for greater well-being. Positive causal networks are stronger when they have more causal drivers or more intense or robust fragments. Optimism can be more intense in itself or more productive of career success, in either case making its causal network stronger.

What the addition of causal interaction adds to objective list accounts is simply that it makes the items on the list more stable and stronger in the psyches of the individuals who instantiate them. Bishop acknowledges that "the part of the network theory that appeals to PCN fragments is akin to the objective list view."[9] The account is then open to the same objections to objective lists as were stated earlier. The lists of goods in actual psychological studies reflect the subjective preferences of the psychologists or subjects, who might want to appear to be of good character. Thus, wealth seldom appears on a list, but spirituality does. At the same time, according to Bishop, what makes a fragment positive is that it feels good or is valued.[10] Once more, if we seek a deeper unifying explanation for why items appear on a list of personal goods, we are led to subjective attitudes, that is, people's values or central desires.

Bishop does have more of an explanation for why items appear on his list of goods than do earlier objective list proponents. His items must have causal powers so as to contribute to self-maintaining networks. But since many states do have such powers, the list will still appear either somewhat arbitrary or bloated. The reason spirituality will not appear on my list of goods is not that it would not make me more optimistic, etc. Perhaps it would if I could be spiritual. But it is not something that appeals to me either doxastically or affectively, not something that fits my belief system, my nature, or motivational set.

[9] Bishop (2015), p. 58.   [10] Bishop (2015), p. 189.

A final recent account that fits none of the categories canvased so far is Sumner's account of well-being as authentic happiness.[11] For him well-being consists in being (judging and feeling) satisfied with one's life when one's level of satisfaction is not based on false information or lack of autonomy, having been brainwashed. My objection to this account echoes my objection to his account of happiness. Satisfaction is relative to how high one sets the bar, to the standards one applies to oneself. But well-being is not so relative. A person with a good career, a supportive family, many friends whom he desires to have, etc., will normally be judged high in well-being even if he is not yet satisfied with his position. While he will have unfilled desires for further advancement, we can assume that many of his central desires are being fulfilled.

The items on any list of prudential goods specify causes of or contributors to well-being; it is the explanation of their presence that indicates to us what well-being is. The simplest explanation will tell us that all the items are rationally desired. It is time then to turn to the explanation that I believe underlies the plausibility of these other theories.

Desire Satisfaction

Well-being is the satisfaction of rational deep desires. Such central desires constitute a person's values. When such desires are being fulfilled, a person's life is going well for him or her, whatever its effects on others. There will of course be significant overlap between this account and the ones criticized in the previous section. The latter would not have been proposed at all if they did not approximate to the correct account. Desire satisfaction brings pleasure (hedonist criterion), and most people desire what is on most objective lists of personal goods.

First, however, directions of explanation differ: pleasure is a byproduct of satisfying desires, and according to the desire satisfaction account, things are personally valuable because rationally desired, not the converse. Second, this is a formal account of what well-being is, not a purportedly exhaustive list of what contributes to or causes well-being. All such lists will be partial or open-ended and relative to different individuals. This

---

[11] Sumner (1996).

radical pluralism in sources of personal welfare indicates the need for a formal, that is, non-substantive, account of what well-being is, such as the one I am proposing. I am not listing sources or things that contribute to personal welfare. I am saying what makes them, whatever they are, contributors.[12]

Other main points in favor of the desire satisfaction account are third, that it implies the strongest link to motivation. We must be motivated to pursue our own well-being because desiring is in part being motivated to pursue what is desired. Relatedly, we have reason to pursue our well-being if reasons are what motivate rational agents.[13] Fourth, the account is fully naturalistic: there is no appeal to mysterious irreducible objective value. Fifth, it explains why items appear on purportedly objective lists: the most plausible items are desired by most people. The objective list advocate might claim equal status here by claiming that there is an explanatory property that unites the various items on his list: they are all valuable. But given, as pointed out earlier, that these lists differ, can we outside judges really discern any such property other than that the items are all desired by the particular creators of the lists?

Finally, the account reveals why personal well-being is subject-dependent. Sources of well-being are relative to particular subjects, differ among them, because different people rationally desire different things. These sources must fit not only their natures, but their motivational sets, what they most centrally desire with relevant information. Pursuing a career in basketball would not promote my welfare because I would not desire to pursue it knowing that it would involve only failure, intense work, and pain with no reward.

Self-interest

Personal well-being equates with rational self-interest. But there are two different senses of self-interest between which we must choose for an account of well-being, and there are intuitions in support of each. A person's broad self-interest can be defined in terms of the satisfaction of any or all of her rational desires (rationality to be spelled out below). In this sense of self-interest, what benefits my children or others I deeply

---

[12] This distinction between enumerative and explanatory theories is now common in the literature. See, for example, Crisp (2006), pp. 122–3; Fletcher (2016); Woodard (2013).

[13] Compare Heathwood (2016). For this definition of reasons, see Goldman (2009).

care about contributes to my welfare as well, since I am very much concerned about their welfare. I take great pleasure in my children's doing very well; it makes me very happy. Surely these are signs that their doing very well makes my life go better. On the one hand, if a loved one contracts a terrible disease, my life goes badly, filled with debilitating anxiety. On the other hand, my loved ones' doing well certainly seems to make my life go better, at least if I know of it, and what makes my life go better contributes to my welfare or broad self-interest.

In addition to intuitions regarding individual cases, other intuitions supporting the equation of well-being with this broad sense of self-interest are first, that it leaves it up to the individual subject what contributes to his welfare. What contributes most is what he most cares about. It cannot be counterintuitively the case that I contribute most to my well-being by satisfying what I less desire or care less about. If I care more about achievement than about having fun, then my life goes better when I achieve than when I party all the time. If I care more about my children than about my money, then my life goes better when I pay for their education.

Second, in this sense of self-interest, if an agent has any rational desires, then she is concerned about or motivated by her well-being. As noted, a person tautologically desires the satisfaction of her desires, and on the equation of well-being with broad self-interest, that satisfaction, if her desires are rational, *is* her well-being. We said that one criterion for an acceptable account of well-being is that it show why we are motivated to pursue it. The desire satisfaction account that equates well-being with broad self-interest comes out on top on this score. We cannot be unmotivated to act on our own desires, since desiring is being so motivated (although such states as depression can override or cancel this motivation).[14] In this sense of self-interest or well-being, we must, if rational, be motivated by our well-being. This is a conceptual truth. This criterion for a satisfactory account of well-being is therefore met as well as it could be.

By contrast, we noted that it is mysterious why we would be motivated to pursue items on an objective list that fail to connect with any of our concerns. In general, our primary motivations do not seem to aim at

[14] See Goldman (2007).

objective value. We do not care about our children or provide for their welfare because we think it objectively valuable to do so, and most of us do not choose our careers or leisure activities on that ground either. Our accomplishments may be of great importance to us, but, unless we are Einstein or Jonas Salk, they matter very little to the world. Very few care whether I finish writing this book, and no one, not even my wife, but I cares whether I become a better tennis player. Yet I will devote many hours to achieving both of these personal goals, although I do not see them as providing great value to the world (well maybe this book, if more than the usual handful of people read it). Once again it is not even a question whether we are motivated to satisfy our deep desires, objective value being irrelevant.

There is also a narrower sense of self-interest according to which what is in a person's self-interest makes essential reference to that person. My children's welfare need not make such reference, while my desire to have a successful career does so refer essentially to me. What I desire is that I have a successful career; your having one does not satisfy that desire (although if you are not a Mafia hitman or Republican politician, I hope you have one too). In this narrow sense of self-interest, one can sacrifice one's own interest for that of others whom one cares about. I sacrifice my narrow self-interest when I pay for both of my sons to go to an Ivy League college. This (supposedly) benefits them educationally and in terms of potential careers, that is, in ways that do not make essential reference to me.

This possibility of self-sacrifice gives intuitive support to equating well-being with this narrower concept of self-interest, since it seems that when I spend every last dollar I have to send my children to college or provide the best care for my old parent, I sacrifice some of my well-being for the sake of theirs. Further intuitive support for this equation lies in the fact that the satisfaction of some other other-regarding desires seems not to contribute to a person's own well-being. I hope that people in Africa don't starve, but their having enough food does not seem to add to my personal welfare. Narrow self-interest is what an egoist pursues for herself, and we might well think that what she pursues is her own well-being. On the other hand, the link with motivation is not so obviously or strongly present here. In this sense of self-interest, a rational agent need not be motivated by his own self-interest: heroes and saints seem not to be, although most people certainly are (but except for Donald Trump, not exhaustively). And what an altruist pursues for another should be the other's broad self-interest, if she seeks for the other what he most rationally cares about.

With intuitions on both sides, if I had to choose between them, I think the stronger case is for equating well-being with broad self-interest. In doing so we have to accept the counterintuitive result that one cannot rationally sacrifice well-being. In fact, one cannot rationally care about things out of proportion to their contribution to one's well-being. In my view, accepting this implication is better than accepting that when one is aware of the fulfillment of what one cares most deeply and strongly about (when this concern is for others), this might not benefit one or make one's life go better. It cannot be the case that my children's welfare contributes nothing to mine, given how much I care about them. And it must be my caring about them that links their welfare to mine.

We could avoid both counterintuitive implications by distinguishing two senses of well-being, just as we distinguish two senses of self-interest, a narrow and a broad. Context might then indicate which concept is in play. But I think it better to retain a single all-inclusive category of well-being that reflects each individual's priorities. We can still take some of the counterintuitive bite out of the rational requirement to pursue or not sacrifice well-being, or at least mitigate this implication, by noting first that one can sacrifice well-being by being uninformed of the full consequences of one's actions, of what it will be like to satisfy one's desire, or by acting in such a way as to sacrifice a more important desire to one less important but perhaps felt more urgently.

More important, we can emphasize that rationally pursuing well-being will sometimes involve sacrificing narrow self-interest for broader concerns. Such sacrifice will be seen as such mainly from the third person point of view, since the person herself will be doing what she most desires, at least until her priorities change. This is not to say, however, that a person placing other-regarding concerns first cannot feel a tension between them and his narrow self-interest. The person who is spending time and money caring for an elderly parent can rightly feel that she is sacrificing *something*, and perhaps something significant despite her admirable priority. What she sacrifices is her narrow self-interest, her self-regarding desires, and these, while less central than her altruistic motives, may be far from negligible. Their sacrifice can be painful and severe.[15]

Rationality and depth

Having resolved this issue by distinguishing personal well-being from narrow self-interest, our work is still just beginning in spelling out and defending a plausible desire satisfaction account of the former. For although we have identified well-being with broad self-interest, we cannot allow the satisfaction of all desires to contribute to it. The satisfaction of some actual desires is not sufficient to contribute to well-being; nor are actual desires always necessary for increases in well-being. Regarding sufficiency, one can desire what is bad for one, such that the satisfaction of the desire detracts from rather than contributing to one's personal welfare. And the satisfaction of some other desires will neither contribute to nor detract from well-being, but remains irrelevant. Spelling out the requirement that the relevant desires be rational and deep will go a long way toward dismissing these apparent counterexamples.

Rational desires must be both coherent and informed. Irrationality in the form of incoherence results in the self-defeat of one's own prioritized aims or desires. Desires are coherent when properly prioritized, so that the satisfaction of some does not block that of others that are deeper and stronger. Deeper desires connect to many others, prominently including instrumental desires for the means to satisfy them, as well as second-order desires that reflectively endorse them. My desire to finish writing this book makes me want to have the time and materials necessary to work on it. And I want to desire to finish the book so that I will be sufficiently motivated to do so. Deeper desires provide reasons for

---

[15] Chris Heathwood (2011) has argued that a person can rationally sacrifice well-being not by distinguishing between broad and narrow self-interest, as I do, but by distinguishing different ways in which a person's life can go better or worse. In one sense a person's life goes better if it is the life he would choose with full information, part of my sense of rationality (information about what it would be like to lead that life). In another sense a person's life goes better if his choice maximizes the satisfaction of his future desires. The former criterion for Heathwood determines the present rational choice, and the latter criterion is the measure of self-sacrifice. Since they can come apart, a person can rationally sacrifice well-being. But I don't see that these criteria will come apart. Even if a person's present desires change in the future (the best case for differentiating the two criteria in practice), relevant information will include the frustration of these future desires, which, I take it, a rational person would not choose.

shallower ones: my desire for good health provides a reason for me to want to exercise; my desire for pleasant sensations gives me a reason to want some chocolate ice cream. Such deep desires contain an implicit evaluative judgment that it would be good for me to satisfy them, while simple and isolated urges may not.

Desires are stronger not simply when more urgently felt, but when they are preferred in contexts of cool reflection.[16] My desire to finish the book is in one sense stronger than my desire for chocolate ice cream, although the latter more often manifests itself as an urge. These two senses of strength can come apart, and strength in both senses can theoretically come apart from depth, making prioritizing a complex matter. But strength in the form of cool and stable preference normally goes together with depth, since one will normally prefer to satisfy a network of connected desires instead of an isolated whim. Since this priority will maximize the total satisfaction of desires over time, it will maximize well-being. We aim at the optimal combination of satisfactions over time, not at the satisfaction of the most strongly felt desire at each time.

In any case, desiring what is bad for one is most often a clear case of desiring something whose attainment will block the satisfaction of a deeper prioritized desire, as when one desires a cigarette at the probable sacrifice of one's health, or to attack one's boss at the sacrifice of one's career. Giving in to such desires is a matter of irrational weakness of will, acting on momentary urges that overwhelm one's more stable preferences. Irrationality is self-defeat of one's prioritized desires, and hence, on the desire satisfaction account, will not contribute to well-being. Overeating at the sacrifice of one's health is an example.

One can also act irrationally or in a self-defeating manner when in the grip of an emotion such as anger or fear (although, as noted, such emotions presumably evolved to promote survival in crisis situations). An employee lashes out at his boss when overcome by anger at the sacrifice of his career and all the welfare attached to it; he fails to apologize when fearing another confrontation. Compulsive behavior, such as compulsive hand washing, has a more complex relation to well-being. Satisfaction of such a compulsive desire might benefit a

---

[16] Such preference is not always revealed by choice of actions, since actions may reflect estimates of success more than strengths of desires.

person in the short run, satisfying her deeper desire to be free of acute frustration, but when repeated over and over it will tend to defeat more central desires, making it irrational, another example of incoherence in desire and action.

The other way in which you can desire what is bad for you is when you are not informed about its nature. Rational desires, those which do not lead to self-defeat, must be relevantly informed. If I desire to climb a ladder without knowing that the rungs are weak, that could be bad for me. But, as Allan Gibbard has shown, the information requirement cannot be spelled out in terms of omniscience: what you rationally desire cannot be what you would desire if all-knowing. Gibbard gives the example (slightly altered) of having knowledge of the operation of people's digestive systems, which would prevent one from going to a dinner with business associates that would benefit one's career.[17] Nor can the appeal be to information that would affect one's choices, which falls to the same example. Instead, the relevant information one must have for rational choice is what it would be like to satisfy the desire in question, for example the desire to go to the dinner. What it would actually be like has nothing to do with the guests' digestive systems.[18]

When one gets what one desired and is disappointed, it is most often because of not knowing what it would be like to satisfy the desire. For example, one desires to go to a dinner thinking he will mingle with the top executives of his firm when only the lowest level of employees will be there. If an agent desires an object because of the way she conceives of its properties, and those properties are other than she conceives them to be, then she is likely to be disappointed when acting to secure the object. The object, as it is, is not what she desires. She desires only the object as she falsely conceives it to be.

Just as I accused objective list accounts of collapsing into desire satisfaction accounts as soon as their rationales are sought or revealed, so the objectivist will say that the information requirement is necessary only to reveal the objective values of the objects desired. Only the

---

[17] Gibbard (1990), p. 20.

[18] Famous proponents of this criterion for relevant information are Sidgwick (1907), pp. 110–11, and Rawls (1971), p. 417. Chris Heathwood (2016) points out that such information can reveal that one does not really desire the object in question, or that fulfilling this desire will block the fulfillment of others that are more important. Thus the criterion of relevant information is a natural part of the desire satisfaction account.

satisfaction of desires for objectively valuable objects will contribute to well-being, he will say, collapsing the desire satisfaction account into an objective list account. The corporate dinner would have real value for the junior executive, and that is why she ought to go and needs to know what it will be like to go.

I reply that the information is required not to reveal objective value, but to reveal what the subject really desires—not the outcome he gets under ignorance of that information, but the outcome he would get from a different object, one with the properties he mistakenly ascribes to the one he has in mind.[19] Furthermore, acting on a desire based on false information is much more likely to defeat a more central desire of the agent. To borrow an example from Bernard Williams,[20] drinking a glass of gasoline thinking that it is gin is likely to defeat one's desire for continued health or life. The person in the example does not really desire to drink the gasoline, but only a liquid that looks like the gasoline but is far different.

As I pointed out in the previous chapter, happiness and well-being will come apart when the subject is mistaken about the object that caused the happiness. When the husband finds out that his wife was cheating on him, this does not show that he was not happy when living in blissful ignorance of that fact. But it does show that he did not have the level of well-being that he thought he had. At least it shows this if he desired that his wife not have an extra-marital affair and thought that this desire was being satisfied. If he had no such desire but sincerely endorsed an "open marriage," then his well-being would not be affected by the new information, lending further support to the desire satisfaction account of well-being. Whether the new information detracts from his well-being all depends on whether it shows that a central desire was being frustrated.

I have now limited the relevant desires in the desire satisfaction account of well-being to rational, that is, informed and coherent, desires. Only the satisfaction of such desires is guaranteed to contribute to well-being. But the limits are not yet sufficient; we must still specify the class of relevant desires more narrowly. The account as stated specifies central or deep desires, those that connect to others, including instrumental desires for means to satisfy them and second-order desires to be the

---

[19] Sobel (2016), p. 268.   [20] Williams (2001).

kind of person who acts on such desires. These desires contrast with isolated whims—shallow, trivial, momentary fancies—and desires from which the agent is totally alienated, the satisfaction of which might not contribute to well-being or benefit a person. Of course some trivial desires might contribute slightly when satisfied, if connected to more central desires. My desire for a piece of chocolate now connects with my more central and general desire to have pleasant sensations, but its satisfaction must also be balanced against my desire not to be fat in calculating its small positive or negative contribution to my well-being.

Further limitations

So much for the characterization of rational deep desires, the satisfaction of which equates with well-being. Two further limitations on relevant desires are required to render their satisfaction sufficient for well-being. First, the desire must exist at the time of being satisfied (or just before). If I earlier desired to teach a certain course but no longer want to do so, then, other things being equal, my teaching it now will not benefit me. The "other things being equal" qualification relates first to pleasant surprises, which will be addressed more fully below. If I find teaching the course pleasantly surprising, it might benefit me despite my not having desired to do so in advance. Second, teaching it might benefit me in other ways, if, for example, I learn things that facilitate the satisfaction of certain of my other desires. It might be instrumentally valuable to teach it, in ways I had not anticipated. But activities unconnected to any present desires will not add to welfare just by having been desired in the past.

Second, the desire must be known to be satisfied in order for its satisfaction to contribute to well-being. When I was 16 years old, I was a high school exchange student in Sweden. I had several friends there, and, caring for them as much as a 16 year-old would, I hoped they would have good lives. I still hope they are having good lives now that I think about it. But knowing nothing of them for many years, their living well now does not contribute to my well-being, although it satisfies my desire. Our earlier intuition regarding the adequately fed people in Africa not contributing to my welfare is captured in the same way if I do not know of them. If I do know of them, then whether their not starving contributes to my welfare depends on how strong and central this desire that they not starve is. If it leads me to adopt complex means to ensure its satisfaction, for example if I travel there to make sure that my contributions are going where they should, then its satisfaction plausibly makes my life go better. If it leads to no action or simply to writing a check with no continued concern, then its satisfaction will be negligible for my well-being.

Interestingly, the frustration of desire is not parallel in respect to the knowledge requirement. It can contribute negatively or subtract from well-being without being an object of awareness. To return to an earlier example, if Sam does not want his wife cheating on him, and, unbeknown to him, she is, then he is not doing as well as he thinks he is. The satisfaction or frustration of desire remains crucial, awareness being necessary only for positive contribution. (Stricter criteria for positive welfare—such is life.)

Surprises and counterfactual desires

So much for sufficiency. Satisfaction of deep rational desires known to exist and be satisfied suffices for contribution to well-being. As for necessity, actual prior desire is not necessary for such contribution. Not knowing anything about a certain research grant, and so not desiring one, if I receive a surprise phone call informing me that I have been given one, I will be made better off. Not knowing anything about golf and not particularly desiring to play, my friend talks me into trying it. I find that I like the game and that the relaxation, exercise, and competition contribute to my welfare. Actual desires do not exist in advance in these cases of positive contribution to well-being and so cannot be necessary.

If we allow that desires can continue to exist while or after being satisfied, then no modification to the account of welfare is required by these cases. But I believe desires exist only for future goods not yet possessed. Of course one can desire that a certain satisfaction continue, but that is a future-oriented desire. If the grant and golf cases cannot be captured by appeal to desires that come to exist only when they are satisfied, then what is necessary is that I would have desired the grant if I had known about it and would have desired to play golf if I had known what it is like, that these counterfactual desires were satisfied, and that I know of their satisfaction.

Hence, not only actual desires, but desires one would have with relevant knowledge can contribute to well-being if satisfied. The objectivist will point out that it is simpler to say that receiving something valuable is what counts here, not some hypothetical counterfactual desire. But for those surprising goods to be personally valuable, I had to be disposed to value them, which is to say that I would have desired them with relevant information. A manual laborer would not benefit from a research grant, and someone who detests outdoor sports, especially slow and often frustrating sports that take skill and patience, would not benefit from playing golf.

It is not the objective value of the grant or golf that contributes to my well-being, but their fitting my motivational set or dispositions. The counterfactual desires that count are counterfactual only because of lack of relevant information. The information would make them real or bring them into existence. A desire I would have if I were a different sort of person does not count. Its satisfaction would not contribute to my welfare. Desires that fit my motivational set are crucial even if counterfactual because of lack of information of the possibility of satisfying them, or of what it would be like to do so.

I have argued that well-being consists in the known satisfaction of existent rational deep desires and of those one would have had with relevant information. I have unpacked the notion of rational desires in terms of coherence and information of what it is like to satisfy the desires. I have spelled out coherence in terms of avoiding self defeat. This account of personal welfare or the goodness of a life to the person living it has handled many of the objections raised to earlier desire satisfaction accounts. These objections point to various kinds of desires whose satisfaction does not seem to contribute to well-being. These include self-destructive desires, shallow desires, those whose satisfaction disappoints, those felt as alien by the subject, those satisfied after death or not known to be satisfied, desires for peace in distant parts of the world, and desires no longer had when satisfied. My account nullifies these purported counterexamples.

I explicitly added to the equation with broad self-interest the exclusion of desires not known to be satisfied. Other counterexamples were excluded by the requirement that the desires be rational and reflective of deeper and therefore more stable concerns. Self-destructive desires are those whose satisfaction would frustrate that of more central concerns, that is, desires that are incoherent with one's broader motivational set. Desires felt as alien will also fail to reflect these concerns that enter into one's self-identification, and they will fail to cohere with second-order desires to be a certain kind of person. The satisfaction of shallow desires will contribute little to personal welfare, or nothing if unconnected to deeper desires. Desires whose satisfaction disappoints are those whose subjects are ignorant of what it is like to act on them, subjects who are not relevantly informed. In all these cases there is no significant satisfaction of deep concerns that anchor other desires in coherent sets. Objections will still be raised, to which we now turn.

Objections

Desire satisfaction?

The first question a critic will raise is whether, having made all the adjustments to the satisfactions of actual desires, all the limitations, and the addition of counterfactual desires, the account remains a desire satisfaction account. It is not so important what we call it if the account satisfies all our criteria for a good theory, and the alternatives do not. But the answer is yes. Existent desires are certainly desires, as are informed and coherent desires, as well as those known to be satisfied. Not counting all actual desires, for example those that are uninformed or self-defeating, those whose satisfaction clearly does not contribute to well-being according to our shared concept of well-being, does not imply that what does count is not the satisfaction of (all the remaining) desires.

The only real question here relates to counterfactual desires, those that do not exist prior to the pleasant surprises that would have satisfied them. But we saw that what makes these surprises pleasant is not their objective value, but is instead relative to the tastes of different individuals, to their dispositions or motivational sets. So what counts is precisely that the individuals would have desired these things with relevant information of what they are like. The required appeal to counterfactual desire satisfaction fits perfectly well with the overall desire satisfaction account of well-being.[21]

---

[21] It might be objected that what makes a surprise pleasant is not always that it would be desired under relevant information, since an ascetic does not desire pleasure. But either the ascetic would not desire the surprise, or he abhors only sensory pleasure, which is not the type of pleasure under discussion here.

Reasons and normativity

The objectivist will still maintain that desires in themselves are too arbitrary to ground true well-being. According to her, we need reasons for those desires whose fulfillment it is rational to pursue. Without such reasons grounded in objective values, all desires have the status of mere whims and urges, whose pursuit might or might not leave us truly better off or flourishing. But there are three reasons why this objection fails. First, as emphasized earlier, our desires cohere in hierarchal structures, the deeper ones providing reasons for others that are instrumental to their satisfaction or are narrower specifications of them. My desire to be healthy provides a reason to desire to exercise, to want to avoid cigarettes, etc. A desire for a successful career is a reason to want to study hard, to choose and pursue a specific career that one can succeed at, etc. A desire for a lucrative career is a reason to choose medicine or law, but not philosophy (in this not best of all possible worlds). Medicine and law are not means to a lucrative career; they are specific lucrative careers.

The objectivist will reply that just as coherence among beliefs does not in itself guarantee truth, something similar is true of desires and well-being. In the case of doxastic systems, some of the beliefs must be grounded in reality or the whole system may be no more than an elaborate fantasy. Likewise, he will claim, some deep desires must connect to objective value or the life in pursuit of them will be relatively worthless. Deep desires may provide reasons for or justify shallower ones, just as some beliefs can justify other ones, but the regress of justification must end, as in the domain of beliefs, with a connection to the independent world, in this case the world of objective values. Without such objective support, desires are said to lack normative force. There is no reason why we should seek to satisfy them, just as there is no reason to believe a set of logically connected propositions with no connection to reality.

But the domains of beliefs and desires are not analogous in this respect. Although incompatible sets of beliefs cannot all be true, incompatible sets of desires can all be worth pursuing by different individuals. As mentioned, my set of desires is very different from those of an investment banker or Tibetan monk, indeed incompatible with theirs in that all these desires could not be collectively satisfied by any individual. But that does not mean that two of us must be wrong to desire as we do; these motivational sets may be equally worthy of directing our lives. There is only one logically consistent realm of facts or truth, but many realizable sets of values worth realizing.

Of the three of us mentioned above, it is true that one or more of us might at some point in a midlife crisis question whether what he is pursuing is really worthwhile. But this need not be construed as asking whether our pursuits have objective value. The objectivist will of course interpret his doubt this way, but his interpretation is not self-verifying. Instead, we might be wondering whether we still really deeply care about what we are pursuing, whether more wealth still grips the banker, or whether getting the next philosophical argument right still grips me (it does). If we do care about what we are pursuing, then we have reason to fulfill these concerns. Once more, we need not ask why we should desire to fulfill our desires. To desire is to desire to satisfy that desire (although this second-order desire might be overridden by other desires).

It remains true that some desires are not worth fulfilling, if they are momentary and trivial or in conflict with more important ones. But this does not imply that all desires require external reasons to satisfy them. While all beliefs must be supported by reasons (even if some of the most significant reasons derive directly from perceptual experience), in the case of desires at the deepest level, one needs no reasons: I do not need a reason to care for my wife and children, to want to have health and a successful career, to want knowledge, to want to avoid boredom and anxiety, etc. In the case of caring for my wife and children, providing a reason would be, in the immortal words of Bernard Williams, "one thought too many." Certainly I do not care for them because I think they have more objective value than other women and children (although they would if there were such a thing). Certainly they would not care to hear such a reason. But even though our deepest desires may lack reasons they do not need, they are not arbitrary, given the way we and the world are. Which brings us to the second reason why the appeal to objective value is superfluous here.

While I have appealed to individual differences in attacking the notion that we should all equally pursue objective value, the objectivist will claim that it is precisely the fact that desires are too socially and individually contingent and variable that makes them lack genuine normative force in themselves. But despite our differences, we have all been shaped by the natural and cultural worlds we inhabit. Our deepest instinctual desires evolved in response to the need for survival in the natural environment. These have morphed into desires for security, for material goods, and so on. Even in these cases, we desire these things to different degrees and in different forms. Most of our desires have also been programmed by our social and cultural environments, which also provide avenues to their satisfaction. And of course collectively over the centuries we have in turn shaped the material and social environments in line with our desires to offer greater opportunities for their fulfillment. Thus, in the worlds we live in, our desires are not at all arbitrary, although they differ from individual to individual. Our natures and cultures largely explain the desires we have, the satisfactions of which are therefore natural candidates for well-being or flourishing in those worlds.

This appeal to a properly restricted concept of human nature and to the nature of the world is perfectly consistent with a subjectivist account of values. There is a world independent of our values, and it has a certain nature or set of properties. And there is a human nature. Even though philosophers appeal to different concepts when invoking it, there are certain properties we all share that typically categorize us as human. Among those shared properties is that of valuing certain things. That we live in different natural environments and cultures partly explains the differences in our values. But the fact that we value very different things is part of what motivates the recognition that values are subjective.

Again, the objectivist will try to turn this argument against us by claiming that social programming is part of the problem, not part of its solution. Before addressing this issue of social programming, I will note the third reason why the objectivist's main thrust misses its mark. She seeks an explanation for why the satisfaction of desires, even informed and coherent desires, must make a life good for the person leading it, and she finds the answer only in desires that track true or objective values. But I take it to be another criterion of good theories that they take explanation only to the level at which they answer more questions than they unanswerably raise.

Thus, if we are scientists, we do not seek to provide explanations for natural laws in supernatural intentions. Appeal to the supernatural raises more questions than it answers, and many of these questions are unanswerable. The same is true of the appeal to objective value, the god of contemporary philosophers, as an explanation (supported only by faith) for our desires. The unanswerable questions here relate to non-natural properties and our mysterious way of purportedly apprehending them. If, by contrast, values are to be natural properties, if objective they still must be independent of our subjective states. And this still raises the question of why we cannot then perceive them out there in the world.

Both divine commands and objective values are supposed to ground our personal values and desires in external standards, but not in any way that we can fully understand. Normativity does not require such standards. Goals that are rational to pursue, those that are coherent and informed, provide reasons and therefore have normative force. Beliefs aim at truth. This aim has normative force in determining how we ought to believe (on the basis of evidence). If we are rational, actions aim to fulfill coherent and informed desires. This aim determines how we prudentially ought to act, how we should act to maximize our well-being.

Objectionable desires

We may return to the problem of socially programmed desires. The objection is that a person can have coherent and informed desires that direct only a subservient life, a life that we would not judge to be good even when all its desires are satisfied. But is the person with mainly servile desires relevantly informed? All our desires are largely socially programmed. But is our only reason for ranking the subservient life low on well-being that it lacks the objective value of autonomy? I would say instead that other lives would be preferred with information of what it would be like to lead them. If the subservient desires would disappear with relevant information, then they are not rational, and that is why their satisfaction does not contribute to welfare.

If they would not disappear when relevant information is provided, this does not yet imply that their satisfaction contributes to welfare. The subservient desires may result from having been in effect brainwashed. There is a difference between social programming and brainwashing. The brainwashed person is incapable of critically reflecting on her desires, such that relevant information cannot be processed or cannot affect her decisions. The brainwashed person cannot meet the information requirement on rationality, and so the satisfaction of her intractable desires does not contribute to her welfare.

Of course the subservient person (the 1950s housewife is the usual model but not always apt—my mother was a 1950s housewife but hardly subservient) is better off for having many of her current desires satisfied than she would be if they went unsatisfied. But if the objectivist thinks that autonomy has objective value, she must agree that subservient people, if not brainwashed, would prefer autonomous lives if they knew what they were like. Hence this counterfactual desire (often actual when alternative lives are conceptualized) provides an alternative explanation for our ranking the servile life low in welfare. To repeat in somewhat different terms, if a person would prefer an autonomous life given relevant (and vivid) information about what it would be like to lead it, then he is not as well off as the autonomous person, and our intuition is accommodated. If he would not prefer such a life after critical reflection (perhaps there are no such people), then perhaps his nature leaves him better off with his current life.

To summarize, my reply to this case can be put in the form of a trilemma. If there is a natural desire for freedom or autonomy in virtually all of us, the subservient person would desire to be autonomous if not brainwashed and with full information of what that life would be like. His present life is then lower in welfare than the life he would like to lead. If the subservient desires result from brainwashing, their satisfaction does not contribute to well-being, since they fail to meet the information requirement and therefore are not rational. If, much less likely, they survive critical reflection with relevant information of an alternative life, then the person is better off satisfying them. In none of these three cases does the satisfaction of subservient desires contribute to a life implausibly high in well-being.

Are we all then badly off, low in well-being, because there are many alternative lives we would prefer with relevant knowledge about them? No, given the relevant comparison classes. As in all judgments of goodness, a comparison class is presupposed. It is always a question of "good compared to what?" When it comes to well-being, the relevant class consists in lives one could realistically live with information of what they are like. I might prefer to be the king of England, but that is not in my relevant comparison class. My life is no worse off for not being English royalty. But if I am subservient, even seemingly willingly so, and would prefer a life of freedom or autonomy if I knew what it is like, and if I could live freely in a reasonably close possible world in which I had that information, then I am worse off for not being autonomous. What about slaves in a society in which the abolition of slavery is still quite distant, requiring, say, not only a shift in attitudes among a sizeable portion of the free population, but also a major war? For any given individual living in slavery, there is still a reasonably close world in which he or his parents were not taken as slaves. It still seems natural to compare him to free persons, as it is not natural or intuitive to compare me to an English king, and that is why we rank him so low in welfare.

A final and seemingly most problematic case is that of a person whose deepest desire is to be miserable. The initial objection is that the desire satisfaction account implies that this person is better off for being miserable, and that implication is unacceptable. The reply distinguishes between several possible (or impossible) cases. First I should say that it is hard to imagine a person who simply desires to be miserable. A person wracked with guilt might desire to be punished as a means to assuage his guilt and feel better after the punishment. This would simply be a case of accepting short-term pain for longer-term benefit, not different except in cause and degree from desiring to go to the dentist. Second, if we can imagine a person who wants to be miserable without any compensating benefit, we would also believe this person to be likely incoherent in her desires, hence not rational, since a miserable person will be incapable of satisfying many other desires she might have. I emphasize again that satisfying irrational desires does not add to well-being.

Finally, a person even more difficult to imagine, who wants only to be miserable. If there could be such a person, perhaps he would be better off being miserable, although it is difficult to know what to say about such a hypothetical person who doesn't want misery as a justified punishment to relieve guilt. As in the earlier mentioned case of Haybron's farmer, this person will be torn between his judgment that being miserable is simply good for him and his feeling miserable itself, or vividly imagining what that is like. A more likely and in fact sometimes actual case is that of a person whose central desire is suicide. But in that case acting on the desire eliminates the subject who could have any welfare to lose. The satisfaction of this desire cannot create well-being in the person who no longer exists.

I have said that a desire to be miserable will most likely conflict with many other desires that a person has and hence not be rational. I added that a person who vividly knows what it is like to be miserable will not desire to be so, again implying that the desire is not rational. But a deeper objection lurks in regard to the person whose only or deepest desire is to be miserable, or, better said, low in well-being, and a stronger response is called for. The objection is that this desire is paradoxical on the desire satisfaction account, and that a theory that generates paradox cannot be acceptable. A lone desire to be badly off, according to the desire satisfaction account of well-being, will leave a person badly off if satisfied and well off if not satisfied. Hence the person will be well off (having his deepest desire satisfied) if not well off, and not well off (having his deepest desire frustrated) if well off—clear contradictions.

The reply is that, since this desire is contradictory, it is also not possible on the desire satisfaction account. As noted earlier, a person cannot simply desire that her desire not be satisfied, since to desire is to desire that the desire be satisfied. (This is compatible with desiring not to have the desire and with having a stronger conflicting desire.) It might be replied that it still seems possible to desire only to be badly off and that this counts against the desire satisfaction account of well-being. But I maintain that the desire will be possible only if the person does not know what he is truly desiring, in the same way that a person can believe contradictory propositions only if he does not put them together or grasp their true meanings. Then too, it will seem possible to have this desire only because it is possible, as I have granted, to have a different desire, a desire to suffer in order to assuage guilt, that is, together with other compensating desires whose satisfaction would leave one better off through suffering. In any case, even if the lone desire is possible, it is certainly not rational, being contradictory, and once more the satisfaction of irrational desires does not contribute to well-being. A person will not then be better off for being worse off: there is no paradox.

If it is accepted that a person cannot desire only to be badly off if she grasps the import of this desire, there may still appear a yet more problematic case. Suppose that A desires only that B be well off, and B desires only that A be badly off.[22] The desire of each is then satisfied only if it is not, on the desire satisfaction account of welfare, again a clear paradox (pardon the oxymoron). These desires seem more clearly possible than in the one person case. The reply again is that these desires will not be rational. This time they will not be rational not because they

---

[22] The case from Skow (2009). He argues that paradox can be avoided by allowing degrees of desire satisfaction, a more complex reply. See also Bradley (2007), who sees the paradox as presently unanswerable.

conflict with some deeper desire of the subject, but because of the relevant information requirement on rationality. If A knows what it will be like to satisfy his desire, he will know that B's only desire will not then be satisfied, and that his (A's) desire will not then be satisfied because B will be badly off. Knowing that his desire could be satisfied only if it is not, he will recognize its irrationality, as we now do. These desires again cannot be rationally had, and seeming paradox once more resolves.

Necessary desires

The programmed desires objection claims that the limitations I have imposed still leave too many desires whose satisfaction is to count toward well-being. The objectivist will also insist that there are too few, in that there are desires a person must have on pain of irrationality and a life that is worse off. A person allegedly must have these desires because of the objective value of their objects, if he is to lead a good life. Concern for one's health, and specifically one's future health, is said to be one such concern. Good health and bodily integrity are held to contribute to well-being whatever one's desires, bad health or serious damage to one's body to detract from it. That is why banging one's head against a wall or cutting off one's finger simply because one wants to is always irrational and detrimental to well-being. But once more I can explain the major part of such intuitions within a desire satisfaction framework and dismiss the rest.

On the one hand, health (or having an intact skull or finger) is instrumentally connected to the satisfaction of so many desires that acts that are detrimental to health without compensating benefits are self-defeating, therefore irrational and detrimental to well-being. But the qualifier regarding compensating benefits is crucial. When none is present or likely, I cannot imagine a person who would not be sacrificing or threatening to sacrifice the satisfaction of some desire by damaging her body or health. And since rational desires must be relevantly informed, a person knowing what it would be like to damage her body or health will vividly know of the sacrifice of instrumentally connected desires, and so will not desire to suffer this damage. Or if she does, this desire will be incoherent with these others, again self-defeating or self-destructive and so not contributing to well-being.

On the other hand, if we include compensating benefits, a person may be so dedicated to a cause or career that seriously risks his health as to rationally lose concern for health. Pursuit of that cause or career might be so central to his well-being that it overrides or cancels out any concern for health. The great tenor Richard Tucker was told by his doctors that continuing to sing opera posed a very high risk of death by heart attack. Knowing that, he continued to perform and eventually did suffer a fatal attack just before a performance. Did he sacrifice well-being? It seems instead that he preserved it as long as he could, given the centrality of his career and artistic achievements in his set of concerns or values. Some might retain the intuition that a person in ill health cannot be flourishing. But flourishing is a matter of degree and again presupposes a comparison class. If minimizing risks to health means sacrificing things one cares far more about, then doing so and leaving oneself miserable is flourishing less.

And many of us do have more pressing concerns. The diminishingly small place of health is typical in the concerns of many great achievers, heroes, and saints (not to mention doctors themselves who eat too much, work too hard, and exercise too little). In the case of heroes and saints, our intuition might be that they sacrifice their well-being for the sake of others. But, as explained earlier, we should rather say that they sacrifice only their narrow self-interest, their well-being or broad self-interest being so closely tied to that of others. In all these cases the connections we see between desire satisfaction, well-being, and health serve to capture our judgments without needing to appeal to objective values or substantive objective constraints on rationality or well-being. For most of us health is a major concern because of its nearly ubiquitous instrumental value. But few of us place it so high among our concerns as to minimize risks to it. Most of us, like the doctors mentioned above, eat too much or too little, exercise too much or too little, or build up stress through work or pursuit of achievement.

If we are concerned about our health now, do we sacrifice well-being by being unconcerned about our future health, a more common case among ordinary young and healthy people? If the answer is yes, and we do then sacrifice well-being without frustrating any desire, this may again appear to imply an objective constraint on rationality and well-being. But there are two replies here. The first again appeals to relevant information. If a person is concerned about her health now and has vivid information in mind about what it will be like to be in ill health in the future, she will become concerned about her health at that later time. Second, since all desires are for things not yet possessed or achieved, since all must therefore be satisfied in the future, to be concerned about health now *is* to be concerned about future health.

How far one's concern extends into the distant future is normally left vague, so that one can sensibly say, "I live for the moment and don't care what happens to me ten years from now." But part of what makes such an attitude irrational is that any such line one draws will be entirely arbitrary. If one knows that one will care about one's health at each present moment, then it will be irrational or self-defeating of one's own desires not to care about and protect one's future health now, since it is the same self who will exist in the future and whose desire will be frustrated by the sickness caused by one's present neglect.

There is no sharp line to be drawn at some future time when one's concern need not be extended back to the present. It is true, however, that the further we go into the future, one's present concern can be discounted by the degree of uncertainty that it will persist. The main point here is that the blow to one's well-being from lack of present concern for the future is still desire-driven, the frustration of one's own future desire. There is therefore no telling objection here from the objectivist. One need not be concerned about one's health at all, except instrumentally if it is necessary for satisfying other desires one has; but if one is concerned about it now and is likely to be in the future, then one must on pain of self-defeat be concerned about future health.

The case is different with a desire I have now but believe I will not have in the future (admittedly a very unusual case). Since desires must exist at the time of their satisfaction (or just before) in order for their satisfaction to contribute to well-being, I need not act now to facilitate a future satisfaction when that desire will no longer exist. A trickier case is a concern I do not have now but believe I will have in the future. If you are currently a young liberal, do you have to act (if possible) to facilitate future elections of conservatives, predicting that, like most old geezers, you will become a future conservative (a prediction already falsified in my case)? Perhaps, in order to maximize well-being over time, the answer is yes, but this prediction and its effect on action must again be discounted by the chance of its not materializing in the uncertain future.

Returning to desires that it is claimed one must have on pain of irrationality, or, what is the same thing, contribution to or detraction from well-being claimed to be independent of desires, next in line of prominence are moral motivations. Many philosophers, beginning with Plato, claim that rationality requires moral motivation and that immoral action or the satisfaction of immoral desires cannot contribute to well-being: a thoroughly immoral person cannot lead a truly good life. This claim threatens our account since it holds that immorality is detrimental to well-being independently of a person's desires.

The latest contributor to this tradition is Paul Bloomfield. His main argument is that self-respect is necessary for well-being and that we must respect others in order to respect ourselves.[23] I reply that we need not respect all others, as morality demands, in order to have self-respect. Perhaps we need to be respected by some others. Even if we need to respect them in order to gain their respect, which is questionable, they can be members of one's tribe, perhaps members who respect harming outsiders or members of rival tribes. If there is some moral incoherence in respecting ourselves while not respecting others, this is not the sort of incoherence that detracts from one's well-being. In this respect it is like the morally incoherent practice of eating pork but not dog meat on moral grounds. The latter instance of moral incoherence does not detract from personal welfare but might well enhance it, if one takes great pleasure in the taste of pork and benefits from the needed protein. Similarly, one can benefit from pleasing the immoral members of one's insular group by imitating them.

To my mind, the numerous counterexamples of successful villains we all know in real life, starting now at the top of our government, are more convincing than any of the arguments could be. Who would not want the life of some notorious billionaires (wouldn't you, even if you would be reluctant to adopt the means to get there)? Be honest, aren't you suspicious of the studies of all the poor psychologists who always conclude that money can't buy happiness (Aesop had a fruitful phrase for that)?[24] Perhaps for most people, and certainly for those better than I am,

---

[23] Bloomfield (2014). See also Badhwar (2014).
[24] Perhaps at a certain level of wealth, more money does not equate with more happiness. Arnold Schwarzenegger is said to have said, "I have fifty million dollars, and I am no happier than when I had forty-nine million."

naturally empathetic people who are well brought up and whose moral instincts have been socially reinforced, immoral behavior would involve personal costs great enough always to overbalance what would otherwise be gains in personal welfare. But first, this is not true of all people, despite our best efforts to morally educate them; and second, for those for whom it is true, the costs relate to undesirable psychological states detrimental to well-being, hardly a threat to desire satisfaction accounts.

Bloomfield's argument that immorality cannot contribute to well-being belongs to a tradition that derives from Hobbes and Hume, being based on prudence or the claim that we are likely to be better off in the long run if we act morally. The claim can be framed in terms of desire satisfaction. Central in most people are desires not only for self-respect, but for reputation and friendship, as well as many others that require social cooperation for their satisfaction. Moral constraint is then claimed to be a necessary means to maximizing satisfaction of these central desires. Immoral behavior is not worth the risk to reputation, self-respect, or open cooperative relations with others. Not only do we need to cooperate with others in order to have our own desires max-imally satisfied, but we normally desire social interaction in itself, all of which is threatened when we seek to exploit other people.

We need not assess other variants of these arguments here,[25] since they are not only compatible with, but assume what I have been advo-cating: a desire-based account of well-being. The claim is that more central desires will be satisfied if we accept moral constraints on our actions. I cannot resist pointing out again, however, that even if prudence requires moral constraint in relations with some people with whom we interact (which explains honor among thieves), moral demands greatly exceed the scope of such prudential requirements. We are morally required, for example, to be concerned about distant future generations, but we have no prudential reason to be so concerned. And although most clever scoundrels are eventually found out and suffer the consequences, it is unfortunately naïve to think this is true of all. Most notorious gangsters come to an untimely end at the hands of their peers; a few die in their sleep in their mansions at a ripe old age. Perhaps the latter were smart enough to reliably predict that it would be so. I suspect that

---

[25] But for fuller discussion, see Goldman (1988), chs. 1 and 2.

many of us personally know of only slightly less villainous characters who led lives full of pleasures and rewards, and know of good people who suffer disasters.[26]

Other Kantian and rationalist arguments for an objective requirement of moral constraint or motivation—arguments that we must universalize our principles of action or grant rights to others if we claim them for ourselves—do not appeal to effects on personal happiness or well-being at all. Hence they are neutral between different accounts of well-being. Moral concern or equal respect for all other persons is supposed to be a requirement of rationality, not prudence. Even if we accept some such argument regarding rationality,[27] we need only grant that irrational action can sometimes benefit a person in order to nullify any threat to our account of personal welfare from this direction. Such occasions might be rare under a narrow conception of rationality, but not under the extended concept to which such arguments appeal. According to this extended concept, morality and rationality can demand the sacrifice of even broad self-interest. Hence immoral actions, while irrational, can preserve or enhance personal welfare or well-being. I have claimed that well-being consists in the satisfaction of only rational desires, but I have assumed a narrower notion of rationality than that embraced by the Kantian. His broader notion is not assumed by him to be connected to personal well-being.

Thus neither kind of argument for a universal requirement of moral motivation threatens our account of well-being. If immoral actions cannot contribute to well-being (I believe they can), this is because they sacrifice other more central desires; if moral motivation is required on non-prudential rational grounds, this has nothing to do with well-being, however construed.

Moral and prudential calculation

A different sort of threat from ethical theory might be seen to arise from claims about the relation between well-being and moral calculation. If, for example, we are consequentialists and think that right actions must aim to maximize the total well-being of all affected, then there is again a

---

[26] Wonderful literary examples are two stories by Mark Twain (1994).
[27] For refutation, see Goldman (2010).

problem for desire satisfaction accounts of well-being. Intuitively, my ardent desire for a new tennis racquet and the amount its satisfaction will add to my well-being imposes no moral obligation on you. It need not enter your moral calculations at all (but feel free to add it). How can this be, given the desire satisfaction account of well-being? If you are to maximize well-being and satisfying my desire would contribute more at less cost than anything else you can do right now, then you are morally obligated to satisfy my desire on the desire satisfaction account of well-being. But you are not so obligated.

The answer is to deny the initial premise. We do not aim to maximize collective well-being and are not morally required to do so, any more than we are required to provide as much pleasure to each other as we can at each moment. What we are morally required to do according to a sensible consequentialism is to respect moral rights, including rights to have basic needs satisfied. However much I desire that tennis racquet, alas I have no right to have others provide it, and they have no obligation to do so. This does not contradict a desire satisfaction account of well-being. It shows only that collective well-being is not the aim or target of moral calculation.

On the other side, some hold that satisfaction of other-regarding or moral concerns should never count at all as contributing to personal well-being. This is equally wrong. It is based on such intuitions as that the satisfaction of my desire for peace in distant parts of the world does not add to my well-being. Certainly it does not serve my narrow self-interest. As argued earlier, whether it serves my well-being depends on how central it is among my concerns, and whether I know of its satisfaction. Well-being equates with (a limited) broad self-interest, in turn with the satisfaction of deep or central desires. When, but only when, the well-being of others is among my central concerns, improvements to their well-being makes my life go better. The depth of my concern for distant peace will be reflected in the extent to which I would be willing to sacrifice other goods in positively influencing its satisfaction (were that possible).

A very different sort of objection derives from my claim that we always aim, indeed must aim, at our well-being. The objectivist will point out that just as we do not typically aim at pleasure, but get it from achieving other things we aim at, so we normally do not think about our desires when deciding how to act, but instead aim to obtain or achieve what we believe has value. The phenomenology of decision making or deliberation, when we aim directly at objects of value to us without thinking about our desires, can be claimed to support an objective list account of well-being.

But aiming at what is of value *to us is* aiming at the satisfaction of our desires, although we normally do not focus on our desires as such in the act of choice. Normally we do not deliberate at all, and yet our more or less automatic actions reflect the priorities among our desires at the time. When we do deliberate, it is because opportunities present themselves with serious pros and cons on each side, and those positive and negative considerations again reflect our existing motivations. We might then seek to further inform our desires or to make their priorities explicit to ourselves. But it is only in times of extreme crisis that we question those motivations themselves, wondering whether we really care about what we assumed we did care about.

Again, none of these processes of deliberation and choice implies a target of objective value. Upon reflection, who would think they were maximizing objective value even in their most serious choices of careers or spouses? Even those few who choose careers as a means of serving others must admit that they do so because they would find such occupations most rewarding. (I am not suggesting a psychological egoism according to which all other-regarding desires are really self-regarding.) You might not think about your desires when acting and making choices in everyday contexts, but surely you don't think about maximizing objective value either. The objectivist has no advantage from the side of the phenomenology of deliberation or choice.

What unifies the various things we aim at is not some mysterious non-natural property they all possess, but the fact that they satisfy our desires or concerns. In choosing, we do not compare quantities of some single independent property, objective value, which we could not measure anyway. Once more the phenomenology of action choice at a minimum supports neither account of well-being over the other. And phenomenology can be metaphysically misleading. It makes us think that colors are purely objective properties (not relational), until science teaches us otherwise. Even if the experience of prudentially deliberating seemed to support an objectivist account of well-being (which it does not), we should be wary of drawing the inference.

Children and couch potatoes

Finally, what are we to say of people (other than servile people discussed earlier) for whom the degree to which their desires are satisfied does not seem to match our judgments about their well-being? On the one hand, we have adults who seem satisfied to watch daytime TV or sports all day, and on the other hand, we have children whose parents rightly choose what is good for them, ignoring their desires for candy and all day play. For such subjects perfectionism or objective list theories will seem better to capture what contributes to or constitutes their well-being. For children, the emphasis seems to be on what facilitates the development of their capacities.[28] For couch potatoes the satisfaction of their desires does not seem to equate with a good life. We seem to know better than they do what is good for them.

These cases are different, not to be analyzed in the same way. In regard to children, do parents really choose for them independently of their deepest desires? As a coach of little league baseball, I saw the unhappy results of parents signing up their children who had no desire to play baseball. In regard to more central desires, children have many of the same broad and deep desires as adults, although they do not specify, explicitly prioritize, or articulate them to themselves. They desire health (not to be sick), to grow strong, to have affection and companionship, to learn many things, and so on. If they lack such desires, this will be because they do not know what it will be like to grow up weak, sick, and ignorant. Of course, despite preferring health and strength, they lack the developed willpower to resist the next piece of candy. But this afflicts many adults as well in slightly different forms, and is beside the point here. Parents rightly seek to prevent self-destructive behavior in their children, but we do the same with self-destructive adults, and such behavior detracts from well-being, reflecting only incoherent or uninformed motivations.

Left on their own, children would often act in incoherent or self-defeating ways, and they are certainly rarely informed of the best ways to satisfy their central desires. More strongly, they are often incapable of gathering or processing information about what it would be like to act on some of their desires. Thus, while they have desires that express

---

[28] Skelton (2016).

basic needs, their desires may well be incoherent and uninformed. And the desires themselves are not fully developed, lacking some of the elements of paradigmatic desires. A child's desire for health or not to be sick, for example, would consist mainly in unpleasant thoughts about illness, lacking dispositions to promote health. But there is still a desire not be sick.[29]

Infants presumably lack even this partial desire, lacking the concept of illness. But even they can plausibly be said to desire nourishment, affection, and warmth, although their concepts of such will be very primitive. In their case, however, we act so as to prepare for the satisfaction of desires they can be reliably predicted to have in the future. Since paternalism is the rule in their case, it is not surprising that we ascribe central desires to them that we are confident they will come to have. We act so as to enable them to have stable, coherent, and informed desires as they grow and mature. Just as moral demands on young children differ from those on adults, so the promotion of their own welfare, or prudential demands, differ also. But the latter can still be interpreted in desire-oriented terms. Thus, even for children, if we care for them, we seek to maximize the satisfaction of their deepest desires over the long run, although it is less obvious than in the case of adults that this is what we are doing in seeking to maximize their welfare.

In regard to the perpetual TV watchers, as in the case of subservient people, we do not rank them high in well-being despite their desires being easily satisfied. I have said that depth of satisfied desires counts in calculating well-being, and this goes a long way toward explaining our ranking in their case. Desires satisfied just by sitting in front of a TV tend to be shallow and unconnected to others. The satisfaction of shallow desires contributes little to well-being. Ease of satisfaction is not a complete explanation for our low ranking of the TV watcher, however, since there are other easily satisfied desires that are not shallow, such as the desire of middle-class people in our society for food. This desire is prioritized and central, both in the fact that it is instinctual and necessary for survival, and in that if it were not easily satisfied, a person would go to great lengths to find the means to satisfy it. Here, however, appeal to comparison classes once more comes into play. In our affluent society,

---

[29] For a full account of the nature of desire, see the appendix.

having enough food to eat constitutes a minimal level of well-being. In the poorest third world countries it would constitute a much higher level. Desires that are very easily satisfied still tend to add little to (comparative) well-being, more so if they are shallow or unconnected to other desires.

In our society, too, some people—Anthony Bourdain types—organize their lives in much more complex ways around their central desire for (a great variety of) food. For them preparing and consuming food is an art. That life would not appeal to me (a lobster and some chocolate ice cream is my ideal meal), but we must be very careful not to substitute our values for those of others whose quality of life we are judging. (I hope I am not simply doing that with the TV watcher or, more likely, the spectator sports fanatic.) At the same time we should not confuse quality of life or well-being with meaning in life. A person with limited deep desires who satisfies them repetitively, or one who skips from one successful project to another entirely unconnected one, might lead a life high in personal welfare, but without much meaning. This distinction remains to be clarified in the next chapter.

Meaning in Life

Preview

Contemporary philosophers, following Susan Wolf, recognize a category of meaning in life distinct from pleasure, happiness, and well-being. They are right about that. Meaning is distinct. It is not a sensation, attitude, or pure feeling, the varieties of pleasure. Nor is it an emotion, mood, or temperament, the forms of happiness. A couch potato can be happy watching TV sitcoms, but he is probably not leading a meaningful life. And while meaning is typically rationally desired and therefore, like pleasure and happiness, a constituent of well-being, it is certainly not the whole, nor even a part for some people.

When we seek pleasure, happiness, or well-being, we are oriented toward the future. We prefer a lesser future good of these types to a greater past amount. But when we look for meaning in our lives, we look mainly to the past and to how it informs the present and perhaps points to the future. Additionally, happiness, pleasure, and well-being all have negative counterparts: unhappiness, pain, and deprivation. Nonsense or senselessness are not negative counterparts to meaning in the same sense. They signify only lack of meaning, while pain is not simply lack of pleasure, and similarly for unhappiness and deprivation. We must seek the meaning of meaningful lives elsewhere than in pleasure, happiness, or well-being.

Other contemporary philosophers note these differences. But when they, and again notably Susan Wolf, characterize meaning in life, their descriptions typically have little or nothing to do with meaning in any ordinary sense. When older philosophers wrote on the meaning *of* life, they typically meant the shared meaning of our lives within the broader context of God's plan for us. The way that human lives fit into God's plan for the universe is similar to the way that events have meaning in relation to the broader narratives of which they are parts, and similar even to the ways that words, our paradigms of meaning, acquire it via their places in sentences or broader linguistic entities. But for modern philosophers who have lost faith in grand religious narratives, there is no shared meaning of life of this sort.

These philosophers speak instead of individuals' meaningful lives, or of meaning *in* life, meaning within lives that might or might not be instantiated in individual lives. But when they switch to this individual perspective, what they posit as meaning is not what older philosophers meant, which was closely related to meaning in its more common forms. They instead tend to equate meaning in life with value or importance, that is, they change the subject. There are two problems with this change of subject. First, there is a perfectly good sense of meaning in life that does not change the subject, that captures something of great value in many lives, and that captures as well much of what the older philosophical question of the meaning of life sought to answer. Second, the dominant newer philosophical approach either relies on the mysterious and superfluous notion of objective value, or it reduces meaning to importance, making it either trivially true that all of us lead meaningful lives, or else false that virtually any of us, save for the rarest of geniuses, do. Value and importance, like pleasure, happiness, and well-being, are again distinct from meaning, or, as I claim in regard to objective value, nonexistent.

I will remedy this situation here by proposing an account of meaning in life that has everything in common with meaning in its ordinary sense. I will argue that lives are meaningful when filled with meaningful events, and that events in lives are meaningful in their ordinary way by fitting into broader coherent narratives. It will be necessary to explicate the nature of narratives and how events acquire meaning within them, and the ways in which, by contrast, lives can lack meaning by being either chaotic or simply repetitive.

Success in long-term goals is a primary source of meaning in the sense I intend, but not everyone seeks a life of gradual and painstaking progress toward the realization of long-term goals. This chapter, similar in structure to earlier ones, after canvassing other accounts and defending mine, will end by considering the ways in which meaning in life relates to value, given that they are not simply equivalent.

Senses and Non-Senses of "Meaning"

Objectively valuable pursuits and importance

Susan Wolf characterizes meaning in life as commitment to objectively valuable projects.[1] Other philosophers agree. Stephen Darwall and John Cottingham, to name two, agree with her that meaning in life cannot derive from purely subjective values, but instead derives from engagement in objectively valuable pursuits. John Cottingham writes: "A meaningful life is one in which the individual is engaged . . . in genuinely worthwhile activities that reflect his or her rational choice as an autonomous agent."[2] Stephen Darwall agrees in this summary of the view: "My normative claim will be that the best [most meaningful] life for human beings is one of significant engagement in activities through which we come into appreciative rapport with agent-neutral values, such as aesthetic beauty, knowledge and understanding, and the worth of living beings."[3] Kai Nielsen appeals to value in a different way. For him a meaningful life is a valuable life: to question the meaning of life is to question the value of life.[4] Kurt Baier also equates a meaningful life with a worthwhile life, although he also seems to recognize that meaning and value are distinct concepts, as indeed they are.[5]

A close usage that at least corresponds to a minor or secondary sense of meaning equates the meaning of or in a life with its importance.[6] This corresponds to the sense of meaning in such locutions as, "His recommendation meant a great deal to me"; "The condolences of his former teammates meant a lot to Jackie Robinson's widow." The paradigms of meaningful lives in this sense are those of such figures as Einstein, Mozart, or Mother Theresa, great and historically significant people who had lasting effects on the lives of others. Their lives were in one sense, from the third person perspective, more important than ours, much as we may hate to admit it. But importance here is precisely importance to other people, the effects of great figures on the lives of so many others. But when we ask the question of the meaning in or of

---

[1] Wolf (1997).

[2] Cottingham (2003), p. 66. For him these are only necessary conditions. What else is needed is a "certain sort of religious or quasi-religious mindset" (p. 85).

[3] Darwall (2002), p. 75.   [4] Nielsen (2008), p. 204.

[5] Baier (2008), p. 109.   [6] Metz (2013), pp. 3, 18.

our lives, we ask it from the first person perspective. We want to know the meaning of our lives to ourselves.

Virtually everyone's life is important to him or her, however important it might or might not be to others (although, as we will see, relationships to others are an important source of meaning to individuals in a more basic sense). A person leading a meaningless life of dull repetition might still think it important to stay alive. His life appears to be important to him but not filled with meaning, indicating that these are not equivalent. In regard to meaning to others, few of us aspire to be an Einstein or think we must be in order to find meaning in our lives. So importance to oneself is not sufficient for meaning, and importance to others is not necessary.

Importance might constitute one sense of meaning because of its synonymy with significance, which, in another of its senses, equates with signification, a more primary sense of meaning. And indeed figures such as Einstein or Mozart have significance in this latter sense as well, in their case signifying or symbolizing to many people scientific or musical genius. But again most of us ordinary mortals cannot aspire to such significance either (much as I would like my life to symbolize philosophical genius). If you are like me, our lives do not symbolize anything to ourselves or others (except perhaps security to our children when they are young). Nor again is this necessary for us to find meaning in our lives.

Bearers of meaning

If signifying is the primary sense of meaning, and our lives do not signify or symbolize anything, isn't this a good reason why philosophers don't attempt to capture anything like this sense in their accounts of meaningful lives? The prototypical vehicles of meaning as signification or denotation are linguistic terms. They have meaning both in virtue of standing in for objects of thought to which they historically have causal connections, and in virtue of their cohering in patterns or sentences. Once again our lives do not have the former kind of meaning or reference: they do not ordinarily denote, refer, or symbolize. Nor is our question about the meaning of the word "life". But the latter kind of linguistic meaning, the meanings of terms such as connectives without concrete referents, which derive their meanings from their places within sentences and inferential patterns, do provide a clue to the kind of meaning within lives that we are after.

The meanings of logical connectives (and, or ...) are exhausted by their relations to other terms and by the inference patterns they allow. They do not denote or refer to concrete objects or actions. Thus not all meaning in the primary sense in which language has meaning depends on such reference, which neither ordinary lives nor portions of lives have. Words have meaning when they cohere in sentences. Sentences can have meaning in themselves, but they can seem to lose their sense, or, on the other hand, acquire deeper or broader significance according to whether they cohere in more extended discourse, whether they follow intelligibly from previous sentences and point to later ones. "Tigers are blue" has meaning in the former sense but is unintelligible in the latter sense when inserted as the last sentence in this paragraph.

This clue to the way lives can have meaning in a primary sense becomes more transparent when we consider meanings of other elements within patterns closely related to the meanings of nonreferential linguistic terms. A close analogy is to elements within artworks. In musical pieces, for example, the musical phrases acquire meaning for competent listeners through their places in developing themes and harmonic progressions, pointing the listeners behind to what prepared for them and ahead in anticipation of developments and resolutions of dramatic tensions. A phrase or theme heard in the recapitulation section of a tonal symphonic movement in sonata-allegro form has a meaning different from its first appearance in an exposition or first section, and from its transformation in a development section. A listener who hears and understands these differences grasps the unfolding meaning of the piece. This meaning derives from internal relations among the musical elements unfolding in an orderly way toward the ultimate goal or final cadence.

An even closer, indeed I will claim a near perfect, analogy is to events in a fictional narrative, a different sort of element within artworks that nevertheless derives its meaning in a similar way. Fictional events in a novel are understood to foreshadow future developments or to fulfill earlier literary promises or resolve earlier dramatic tensions. The meaning of Huckleberry Finn's refusal to turn in his runaway slave friend Jim relates to their earlier developing friendship on the raft and to Huck's resulting but nonself-conscious moral awakening, ironic in relation to Huck's own understanding of his action. When a reader grasps these relations, she interprets and understands the meanings of the fictional events in terms of their roles in the narrative structure. I will claim that meanings of real life events are analogous and that lives are meaningful when filled with meaningful events. Before pressing this analogy and noting relevant differences, an objection that will immediately arise must be cleared away.

The Meaning (or Lack of It) of Life

As just indicated, I will provide an analysis of the meaning of events within lives and claim that lives are meaningful to the extent that they are filled with meaningful events. This will then be an account of meaning *in* lives, and not of the meaning *of* life itself, or as a whole. While this is a familiar distinction within the contemporary literature on the topic,[7] and while Susan Wolf and those who follow her are content to propose answers to the former question and dismiss the latter one, other more traditionalist philosophers and religious thinkers, including those who focus on the importance of lives instead of on commitment to valuable projects, will accuse me of changing the subject, as I have accused them. It is therefore necessary briefly to reiterate telling objections to the once popular answers to the more traditional question. I will also claim that answering the newer question of the meaning in life should assuage the worries that prompt the older question of the meaning of life.

Grand myths

Traditionally, the solution to the problem of the meaning of life appealed to the notion of a broader plan or purpose or grand scheme into which each person's life fit. A life was considered meaningful either by fitting into God's plan for it in His broader plan for all humanity, or for the universe as a whole, or by playing some role in a grand, eschatological, historical myth. Like particular events, a life as a whole can acquire meaning only in relation to a larger whole of which it is a part, in terms of its relations to other parts of that whole, in this case temporal parts occurring earlier and later in overarching religious or historical narratives. Our lives were supposed to have meaning by fitting God's purpose or plan that involved all of us, or by fitting some naturalized

---

[7] Perhaps first drawn by Kurt Baier (2008) (reprint of lecture from 1957).

but still mythological fated or inevitable rational course of historical development, again involving some final purpose or goal, for example the Hegelian goal of Absolute Spirit or the Marxist final end of communist society. Life within each historical stage, and especially in the revolutionary transitions, was to have meaning in relation to the place in history of those stages.

This notion of meaning in terms of purpose or plan does once more capture an ordinary, if again secondary, sense of meaning that we invoke when we ask what people mean by various actions or remarks. "What did he mean by interrupting her speech, by running out on the field in the middle of the game, by saying that he would not run for office?" We raise such questions when we do not understand the point or purpose of the action or remark, the broader plan into which it fits. We want to know what broader concern of the agent makes her action intelligible to us or rational for her, what she intends and how the intention was rational or fit her broader concerns. The denial that one will run for office might mean either that one will not run, or that one will when the proper time and support come, depending on the agent's intention and broader plan.

When we ask for the meaning of a remark in this sense, it is not that we do not understand the language, but that we do not see the point or significance of the remark in the broader scheme of things, how it relates to an ongoing conversation or figures in the speaker's broader purposes. And we can understand the meanings of nonlinguistic actions in the same way, by understanding the broader intentions or purposes behind them, the plans into which they fit. If the politician's plan is to elicit vocal or monetary support, then what she meant by saying that she would not run for office was that she needed to see support from others before throwing her hat into the ring. If her plan was to stay out of politics in the near future, then she meant something different.

So the traditional answer to the meaning of life captured a quite ordinary and natural sense of meaning, as opposed to some aforementioned answers to the more contemporary question of meaning in life. The traditional answer to the traditional question nevertheless makes little sense to us nonreligious and non-Hegelian or non-Marxist inquirers. First, if there is no God, or no final goal at which history aims, these answers are nonstarters. There are no grand external plans into which ordinary lives fit. Meaning must derive from elsewhere if there is to be any.

Second, it is far from clear that fitting a plan of some other being or force, a plan of which we have no knowledge, could provide our lives with meaning. If I play some unwitting role in some long range plan of yours, could that bring meaning to my life? There might then be a meaning of my life to you, but not to me as I am living it. How is it different if the plan belongs to an all-powerful supernatural being or (metaphorically) to a blind historical force? One might attempt to give one's life as a whole meaning by becoming wittingly and fanatically devoted to some actual global movement or revolution, but that is not an option that would appeal to most of us (more on such fanatics later). But in the absence of knowledge of some all-encompassing plan, being a part of it could not mean anything to an agent herself. Perhaps in the religious story such knowledge is supposed to come after death, but that could be of little comfort to a person who wants to know the meaning of life now.

The cosmic perspective

The problem is not just lack of knowledge of any grand plan into which one's life fits. Given the size of the universe (10^{24} planets), all of which is part of God's plan, no individual could be more than an extremely miniscule (to put it mildly) tool in that infinitely larger incomprehensible plan, a not very uplifting kind of meaning. Such narratives could only swallow up the lives of the unwitting pawns who barely enter into them. As others have pointed out, the cosmic perspective of the universe through all of time hardly reveals an otherwise invisible meaning to our lives. Instead, thinking of that perspective seems to rob our actual projects and relationships of any meaning they might otherwise have.[8]

In the long run we are dead for a very long time, and as our lives fade into the very distant past, they will seem to have made no difference that matters. Their meaning, if they ever had any, will fade as well. Most of us will be remembered on rare occasions by our grandchildren, and after that not at all. And, if it's any consolation, those geniuses who are remembered longer still occupy less than a speck in cosmic time. Even the effects of Einstein's scientific revolution or Mozart's perfect music will disappear before or with the human race in the run of cosmic time.

[8] See, for example, Nagel (1971).

One life will matter as little, and mean as little, as another. If it is in general true that reflective distance and a wider perspective provide a more objective view from which to interpret events, and if that generality holds true here, that only shows that there is no meaning of our lives, certainly none that all our lives share through our role in the whole course of (God's plan for) the universe.

Loss of faith

In any case, to us to whom the question of the meaning of life might seem pressing, it will at the same time seem senseless, since there is no longer any super narrative scheme beyond us into which our lives can fit and in terms of which they can have a purpose. In the modern and postmodern ages we have lost faith in these religious and secular grand narratives that provide external purposes or plans for our lives. ("We" here refers to the majority of the philosophically oriented people who are reading this. If you are not one of them, if you think you know God's plan for you, thank you for reading and skip to the next paragraph or next section.) Teleological explanations of the course of history have given way to causal explanations. The human race itself is now seen to be the product of blind physical forces. There is no grand plan for the lives of ordinary people, but perhaps only for those fanatics who devote their entire time to a single cause.

The causes to which we normal people commit ourselves are self-chosen, diverse, and not all-consuming. Our purposes are the purposes we adopt and to which we devote ourselves. So we have lost faith also in the idea that life itself (or all lives) has a single purpose that could give to each the same sort of meaning. There is no single meaning of life. The question for some has become only a setup for the punchline of a joke. For others, the question might seem to become pressing just when this type of meaning appears to be lost, just when it cannot be answered. Thus, some philosophers will dismiss the issue entirely when they cannot accept the older responses to it. For others, myself included, the question in a somewhat modified form can be given an answer that should alleviate the angst from which it arises.

Meaning in Life

Although the question of the meaning of life has no answer, our lives can still seem meaningful to us as we live them, even to us atheists for whom meaning cannot derive from belief in God's plan. This meaning is internal to our lives as we live them. But if internal, and if meaning is relational (something means something else to someone), such meaning must attach to aspects or episodes within life. It makes sense to ask for the ground of this sense of meaning that we feel in our daily lives, or sometimes lose. Philosophers are right to seek the answer to the question of meaning in life. And the answers they have given—in terms of importance, valuable projects, or purpose—while changing the subject unnecessarily, do again provide clues to the right answer.

The meaning of events

The answer lies in the meanings of events in our lives that affect them, parts of our lives that confer meaning on the whole. We must give an account of how such events acquire meaning instead of looking first for the meaning of the whole of life. That our lives were supposed to have meaning by having a purpose or fitting a larger plan provides an analogy for the meaning of events within our lives. And events are meaningful when they are important and valuable (or disvaluable) to us, although their meaning in the primary sense does not derive from their import- ance or value alone. We may now proceed to the full explication of meaning in life, picking up on these clues as we go.

As noted, meaning, unlike value or importance, is always a three-term relation: something means something else to someone.[9] Nothing is meaningful in itself: x means y to z because z perceives x's relation to y. For an event to mean something in someone's life, it must mean some- thing to a subject who experiences it in some way. It will mean something to her only if she takes note of it, and she will take note of it only if it is important or has positive or negative value for her. But importance and value are two-term relations (something is important or valuable to someone), necessary conditions for events to have meaning, but not identical to their meanings. An accidental discovery that turns out to be important will not be meaningful to the discoverer unless he recog- nizes it as having such effect.

Important events are meaningful in virtue of their relations to other events preceding and following them. Their meanings derive from the outcome-directed sequences of events of which they are parts. Like

---

[9] I am not speaking here of speaker's meaning, which involves higher order intentions and more than three terms.

words, events are meaningful when they cohere in intelligible temporal patterns. We make sense of the present situation in terms of its past and what it seems to aim at. We make sense of the past by structuring it into a coherent pattern aiming at certain ends, outcomes, or developing relations. And we conceive of possible futures as outcomes of past events and present intentions.

Meaning derives from the relation of an element to something outside it to which it points for some observer. In the case of events, these relations are typically temporal. The most meaningful events are those that initiate, culminate, or change the course of an unfolding project or relationship. My marriage ceremony, the births of my children, the first copy of my first published book, my moves to new jobs and locations—these initiating and culminating events remain most meaningful to me. The temporal relations they mark are at least partly causal, and once more causal relations underlie an ordinary way in which we ascribe meanings to events or objects. Clouds mean rain; smoke means fire; spots mean measles or mean that fever will ensue. Thus causes mean their effects; effects mean their causes; and common effects of single causes can mean each other.

Events lend themselves to meaningful interpretation partly through their causal relations, a cause pointing the observer to its effect or vice versa. Causal sequences of events, especially those that constitute intentional actions of agents, in turn acquire meaning by relating to other sequences or to broader concerns of the agents, who unite these actions in orienting them toward broader goals. The analogy with words and sentences is again relevant here. Sentences lend meaning to words but can themselves seem senseless when lacking in or conflicting with broader contexts. Intentional actions, while making intelligible those more basic movements that enter into them, can in themselves seem senseless unless related to broader purposes or goals. My writing the previous sentence makes sense as the culmination of the paragraph, not much sense otherwise, or as the last line of *Huckleberry Finn*.

Just as the meaning of an action does not derive from the objective value of the goals pursued, so it does not derive from the nature of the activities in themselves. In itself shooting a ball through a hoop makes no more sense than throwing it as high as one can into the air; hitting a ball over a net is no different as an isolated action from hitting it into a net. These activities become meaningful when nested in a connected set of concerns validated by a social structure that orients them toward various broader goals. Throwing a ball through a hoop, as opposed to high in the air, can be at the center of such concerns as developing physical skills, competing, winning, earning respect of peers, creating school spirit, and having a lucrative career. That is why it can be a part not only of such long range goals, but even of a life plan for those with some chance of success at it. For Lebron James it is the outcome of countless hours of practice, part of winning a game, making the playoffs, being rich and famous. For me it is just a relaxing bit of exercise. And these various goals into which the activity can fit relate it to many others and thereby render it a meaningful activity, while throwing the ball in the air is a strange waste of time.

One can also question the meaning of overall patterns of such activities. Are they cumulatively leading anywhere (toward a career, fame and fortune, college admittance, etc.)? Do they amount to—that is, mean—anything? My repeatedly throwing a ball through a hoop may again be a waste of time (if not a form of needed exercise or relaxation), if I do not plan to play or have no chance of playing in basketball games. But for one practicing for games, the number of repetitions may later become highly meaningful, leading to making or missing the crucial game-on-the-line foul shot. The meaning of any such sequence of events again depends entirely on its relation to other sequences that culminate or initiate, foreshadow, or continue it. If then, as I have suggested, a meaningful life is one filled with meaningful events, such a life would consist in intelligible successions of events, giving meaning to each event by relating it to others in an unfolding narrative that makes sense of each as a precursor of the next and culmination of the prior.

Narratives

I have now introduced the central concept of a narrative: meaningfulness in life is a matter of narrative intelligibility. Narratives are precisely what explain events by fitting them into fully intelligible sequences. They usually refer mainly to sequences of intentional actions and events that influenced them in the settings that prompted them, indicating why they occurred and what they led to. These events are related causally, but in the case of intentional actions, not only causally. Later actions are not just causal effects of earlier ones, but fulfill the promises or goals of the earlier ones. They therefore explain the earlier ones that were intended to lead to them, as the earlier ones explain them. Narratives, as representations of sequences of intentional actions, aim, as the actions themselves do, at their final outcomes, conclusions, or ultimate goals. They are therefore understood teleologically as well as causally, affording them a greater intelligibility than that of mere causal sequences. At any point in a narrative understanding, readers or observers look forward to likely outcomes as well as backward to causes. The goals at which narratives aim, projections of which are required for full understanding as they unfold, in turn express the values of the agents and narrators.

The paradigms of intelligible narratives are not full descriptions of sequences of events from real life, but fictional stories. Here all the characters and events exist only to fulfill intended goals in the service of aesthetic or literary values. To interpret these characters and events is to show how they serve such values, and the relations between them are always fitting objects of such interpretation. In a well-constructed fictional narrative, all events are therefore meaningful, even if only as needed diversions from main themes. And all the minor characters function not only to move the story along, but as contrasts to the main characters, revealing their psychology more clearly through these contrasts. In *Pride and Prejudice* (to cite just one most popular canonical example I hope you have read), Elizabeth Bennett's sisters play just such roles. Jane's connection to Bingley and Lydia's elopement with Wickham carry the story forward, and all three sisters in their stunted moral developments (despite Jane's natural kindness, she lacks moral perception and discrimination) contrast in different ways with such development of the two main characters throughout the novel.[10] This kind of structure is typical in maximally coherent literary fiction.

In literary works all the characters and events exist and take place for aesthetic purposes, filling out themes that are both substantive and formal in uniting different parts of the stories. Sticking with our example, the theme of moral development in *Pride and Prejudice* both formally unites different events and phases in the story and substantively reveals Jane Austen's theses as to the nature of such development, how its catalyst can consist in cooperative interaction with people having different

---

[10] Even Jane, who is a kinder person than Elizabeth in seeing only the best (often unwarrantedly) in people, lacks the ability to make moral discriminations necessary to react properly to complex situations.

backgrounds and perspectives, etc. In real life there typically are no such single unifying themes running throughout.[11] Real life is not so aesthetically neat. Not every event that befalls us or even every action we initiate is part of a larger theme or coherent pattern. Many events in the real world can be explained only causally, including those over which we have no control but which may influence the course of our lives.

Nevertheless, even such events, if included in our real life narratives, are included because they lead to further developments in our ongoing stories, their inclusion being explained teleologically, even if their occurrence admits only of causal explanation. The meanings of even such external events depend on how we react to them. The explanation of real intentional actions is always forward-looking, referring to the ends of the actions, as well as backward-looking to external and internal causes. Such actions are themselves both effects and causes aimed at future outcomes. And, like fictional events, they express the values of their agents, in real life not typically aesthetic values, but ends prudentially or morally valuable for the agents to pursue. Life contains no single unifying themes, but many interrelated as well as independent stories, each with their own themes and subplots.

Narratives capture the meaning of events in our lives. They do so by explaining the events in teleological or forward-looking as well as causal or backward-looking terms. The most meaningful events, for example marriage ceremonies, are pivotal elements in the most extended narratives. A marriage culminates a premarital relationship and hopefully begins a much longer chapter. Backward- as well as forward-looking explanations are necessary for understanding the actions of other people, grasping their meanings. We understand the actions of others best when we see them as emerging from their characters, from their sets of values as reconstructed from our knowledge of their narratives up to the present context. In so far as we know their narrative histories, what they care about, what is meaningful to them, we can infer their dispositions and predict their actions. Such prediction is necessary for successful social interactions, and various social norms and the roles they govern facilitate it, as will be explicated further below.

---

[11] Compare Lamarque (2007).

Selves

Do we also understand ourselves in such terms? In large part, yes. Many philosophers conclude that the self itself is a narrative construction. This is only partly true. There is both a basic pre-narrative self and a higher order narratively understood self, having character and personality. When I act out of character, in one sense it is not I who acted, but in another more basic sense it is indeed I who did it.[12] This more basic sense, applied in deciding criminal responsibility (except in cases of insanity and coercion), applies both to others and oneself. In a criminal court we want to know first who pulled the trigger, before we ask whether the act was in or out of character.

In the case of others, it is mainly bodily identity, not psychological continuity or narrative intelligibility, that thereby determines who did the actions and is responsible. From the first person perspective, I am aware of myself as the pre-narrative subject of my narratives, as well as of lapses in them. I am aware of myself as the subject of all my experiences, whether coherent or not, from my unique perspective, experiences to which I as their basic subject have unique access. Not only did this basic I do certain things out of character when I was "not myself," but it is this self who I fear will suffer in the future and die, no matter how much my character might have changed by then. This basic self, not requiring knowledge of narratives, is the primary object of my hopes and fears (although I might also fear becoming a different and worse person), as well as the initial locus of my responsibility.

Just as there is a basic pre-narrative self, so there are pre-narrative events that we witness and pre-narrative experiences that happen to us. These events involve objects that are conceptualized, but not necessarily in narrative terms. All ordinary experience is immediately conceptualized or categorized based on prior experience and culturally imposed categories, but such experience will fade or be forgotten if not made part of a story. The stories themselves will be of greater or lesser length or importance. While the dentist is drilling, the patient will rarely be thinking in narrative terms, although he will conceptualize his experience as pain. In retrospect, there is likely to be a short story with a sad

---

[12] For similar accounts of levels of selfhood, see Schecterman (2007) and Zahavi (2007).

beginning in a cavity and a happy ending in a pain-free filled tooth. Longer ongoing narratives will select events as they occur and determine their interpretations. Events acquire personal meaning by being incorporated into our personal narratives. At the same time, when events happen as consequences of our intentional actions, they come already with narrative meaning.

There are again parallels and differences between real life and fictional narratives. Words and sentences in a fictional text are read with ready-made meanings and are then interpreted first by figuring in the story, and then in terms of themes that the story instantiates. As in real life experience, there is pre-interpretive text to be interpreted, possibly in different ways. In fiction, aesthetic criteria ideally determine the shapes of the stories, into which all the narrated events fit. As noted earlier, real life experience is far messier and more recalcitrant. But in real life too aesthetic criteria and master narratives, often from fiction, influence and help to determine the stories we tell. We want our autobiographical stories to be interesting or amusing, and this often leads to distortion and contrived meanings, which may gradually take on the appearance of truth, even to ourselves. We tell and hear stories of military service, achievement in sports and intellectual pursuits, economic success, and so on. We imperfectly pursue such narratives in our lives, and the stories we tell of these pursuits are often somewhat slanted toward an aesthetic ideal, our resulting self-conceptions falling somewhere between fiction and reality. On the negative side, when there is blame to be assigned or guilt to be acknowledged, as in divorce cases, we see how the same events receive very different interpretations fitting different self-conceptions.

I have said that I fear the demise of my pre-narrative self: I fear that this body will deteriorate and die. But what I also fear in regard to death is the end of my projects and relationships, probably premature ends, and my future lack of knowledge, for example, of how my grandchildren's characters will develop. This again refers to the higher sense of self understood in narrative terms. I conceive not only of others, but of myself as having a character, or a relatively stable set of behavioral dispositions. I recognize certain commitments deriving from my past that I, as a person of integrity, will fulfill. If I have contracted to write an article and then lose interest in the topic, I will still write it because I do not want to be the type of person who reneges on commitments made. These dispositions and commitments, resulting in part from past experiences, reflect a self that is captured in narrative terms.

I believe that I, as well as others, have a coherent personality that projects my past choices into future actions. This belief affects my choices, such as the choice to write the article I no longer want to write. But the extent to which this belief is true has been a hot topic in recent philosophy and psychology. I will not take a stand on that debate here, although I and others have argued elsewhere that attacks on the notion of stable character are often supported by far too quick inferences from questionable and highly artificial psychological experiments.[13] Regardless of whether individuals' reactions are more reflective of stable character traits or current situations, it is the narratively expressed and understood self that reflects what is meaningful in one's life, which events have meaning that can influence, however strongly, one's future decisions.

Paradigms of Meaningful and Meaningless Lives

Repetition

To get a better grip on the types of lives that are most and least meaningful, that are most or least filled with meaningful events, we can at this point find intuition pumps in recognized paradigms of meaningful and meaningless lives. The paradigm of a meaningless life in the philosophical literature is that of the mythical Sisyphus, first referenced by Richard Taylor.[14] Sisyphus must endlessly roll a stone up a hill, only to see it roll back to the bottom. This endlessly repetitive activity with no point relates to nothing but itself. That we see it as therefore meaningless confirms the idea that meaning in life events consists in relations to other events deemed important by the subject. Mere repetition without variation or development is the first paradigm of meaninglessness.

According to Taylor, if Sisyphus suddenly developed an urgent desire to roll the stone, if he willingly committed himself to the task, then the activity and the life built around it would acquire meaning for him. But critics rightly respond that this life of mere repetition is no more

---

[13] Goldman (2013), pp. 183–4.   [14] Taylor (2008), pp. 256–68.

meaningful for being engaged in willingly. The altered Sisyphus might find life far less burdensome, might even be happy or find pleasure in rolling the stone, but his life would be no more meaningful for that. If Sisyphus thinks that his behavior is meaningful, he is simply mistaken. It might be important to him, but it relates to nothing else and has no point.

The satisfaction of a single desire is not sufficient to confer meaning on an action in any ordinary sense in which we understand meaning. Satisfying whims does not provide meaning in life. At the beginning of this book we saw another character who similarly illustrates the independence of pleasure from meaning. Don Giovanni leads the ultimate life of pleasure and is perfectly happy doing it, yet Kierkegaard's attack on his purely aesthetic existence is in large part for its lack of meaning. Since one sexual conquest is the same as another to Don Giovanni, he again leads a life of mere repetition (which is not to say that the fictional story itself lacks meaning or point).

The contemporary counterparts to the ancient Sisyphus and Medieval Don Juan are the couch potato who spends day after day watching TV soap operas, sitcoms, or baseball games, and the addicted shopper who makes trip after trip to the mall. Like the altered Sisyphus and Don Giovanni, these characters willingly engage in their pointlessly repetitive behaviors, might derive pleasure from laughing at the sitcom jokes or buying a new dress, might even be content or at least not unhappy, but they are still leading meaningless lives. That judgment again persists no matter how content these characters seem, no matter how much pleasure they derive from their addictive activities.

It might be objected that the soap opera watcher experiences the events in the extended stories, all of which have meaning if they are well written, and that his life is therefore filled with meaningful events. If we nevertheless retain the intuition that this person's life lacks meaning, this would refute the analysis of meaning in life in terms of experienced meaningful events. But of course we are speaking of fictional meaning, meaning in the story and in the lives of the fictional characters, not meaning in the life of the TV watcher. Spending an entire life reading fiction and doing nothing else is not a plausible example of a meaningful life either, however well constructed the fictional stories are, however meaningful the events in those stories. Meaningful events in the stories are not meaningful events in the lives of the readers, unless they influence the readers to change the course of their lives. A final well-known similar example is the meaningless work of the assembly line worker, who once more simply repeats the same motions without being mindful of their place in the manufacture of the final product.

Incoherence

Events in life lack meaning not only when simply repetitive, but when incoherent in sequence or seemingly pointless from the agent's perspective, when they seem to be going nowhere, even if they do not simply repeat. Not only boredom, but frustration and confusion are signs of lost or lack of meaning. Disintegration and incoherence, as well as mere repetition, destroy meaning. Boredom from mere repetition provides no other events to which to relate; frustration and confusion reflect lack of direction or meaningful progression, disconnected events with no continuity, no matter how varied. As is not unusual, Shakespeare best captures both pathologies in Macbeth's most famous speech:

> Tomorrow, and tomorrow, and tomorrow,
> Creeps in this petty pace from day to day,
> To the last syllable of recorded time;
> And all our yesterdays have lighted fools
> The way to dusty death. Out, out, brief candle!
> Life's but a walking shadow, a poor player
> That struts and frets his hour upon the stage
> And then is heard no more: it is a tale
> Told by an idiot, full of sound and fury,
> Signifying nothing.

Clearly Macbeth laments the meaninglessness of life: its tedious repetition in the early lines, its incoherence in the later. Life aims only at "dusty death," not coherently at any other goals that could bestow meaning on it. The person who flits aimlessly from one thing to the next, no matter how enthusiastic or "full of sound and fury," lacks meaning in life equally with the one stuck in a rut of endless repetition. Any life lacks meaning that lacks direction or intelligible progression, narrative intelligibility. Of course, Macbeth was wrong about his own narrative: more than in the life of any real person, there was a logic to all the narrated events in his life. They led inexorably in the direction of his tragic end. Meaningful events lead cumulatively to good *or* bad outcomes.

Macbeth's powerful lament also suggests by contrast what a meaningful life could or should be, what, according to him, it pompously purports or pretends to be (in the person of a poor player strutting on the stage). If we want examples of lives filled with meaning, we need not appeal to such paradigms as Einstein or Mozart, who spent their entire lives revolutionizing physics or bringing music in the classical style to its highest point, but who seem entirely inaccessible as models we could emulate. We need only alter the examples of meaningless lives so that they no longer seem so.

It is then revealing to compare the life of a professional fashion designer or baseball player to that of the consumer or fan. Winning the World Series can meaningfully be at the center of the player's concerns because it relates to and indeed organizes many other activities and concerns—desires for accomplishment, a successful career, and wealth, for example—and it culminates years of endeavor. All the practice aimed at that end also thereby acquires meaning. For the fan there are no such organizing relations; the new season of passive watching simply begins shortly after the previous one ends. The actions and events in his life are simply repetitive instead of cumulative. As we saw earlier, however, even mere repetition can become meaningful when related to a broader context or goal. Practicing free throws seemingly endlessly acquires meaning when it aims at, and especially when it achieves, the clutch points at the end of a game. And even for the fan, games within a season can be meaningful (even if not sufficiently to make his life meaningful), unless again they form no coherent pattern, but seem to be simply random wins and losses.

Meaning and value

Now alter the life of the baseball watcher characterized as meaningless. Imagine that the person organizes a whole set of concerns and activities around watching baseball games. (We can also imagine that he does not neglect his family, that he has sufficient income to indulge his passion, and so on, so that moral questions do not interfere with our judgment.) He scrupulously plans trips to various stadiums in different cities, collects souvenirs from these trips, collects and trades baseball memorabilia, gradually building a collection that reveals the history of the sport, memorizes statistics from all the games he watches and from the sport's history, follows trades, potential trades, salaries, and so on. Furthermore, his expertise and involvement in the sport increases over time. A believer in objective value as necessary for meaning in life would still brand such a life meaningless (assuming she knows and cares nothing about baseball) and would claim further that what makes it so is not the lack of internal relations among its activities, but its lack of an objectively worthwhile project.

I disagree. This life certainly does not fit my taste, although I am a sports fan, but the events in it do have meaning. As with any bearers of meaning, they point outside themselves and become intelligible in terms of their relations to these referents and to overall plans and goals. As events in a complex ongoing project, they refer back to earlier events whose promise they fulfill or forward to future events for which they prepare. They therefore have meaning for the person leading this life. They might lack meaning for us, if we would not deem them important enough to keep track of their relations.

Of course, this type of meaningfulness is a matter of degree, and it remains true in our modified example that each new baseball season simply begins a new cycle much like the previous one. But there is repetition in any life, perhaps necessary for stability and security, and in this one there is also progression as the memorabilia and experiences in different locales add to the earlier ones. The meanings that accrue here may seem to lack objective value, but I will have more to say about that critique later. This life may seem to lack meaning when viewed as a whole, but then so do other lives when viewed as a whole from a broad enough perspective, as noted earlier. Events in such lives can still have meaning when lived, although the meanings they have will appeal or fail to appeal to different observers.

Sources of Meaning

Long-term goals

Intentional actions and meaningful events are themselves temporal: they have beginnings, middles, and ends. If all intentional actions also involve means–ends relations, aiming at ends or culminating means, if meaning accrues to such relations, and if we are all acting intentionally almost all the time, doesn't that imply that all our lives are therefore filled with meaningful events, and therefore all equally meaningful according to my account of meaning in life? No, because these intentional actions in turn acquire meaning by relating to each other as episodes fitting plans in the pursuit of longer-term goals. Meaning in life is a matter of degree—we can ask how meaningful a life appears to be. Greater or deeper meaning accrues to events or actions the broader the intentional contexts in which they are embedded.

The more coherent a person's concerns and activities aiming to satisfy them are, the more meaningful her life will seem to her. Deeper, more important, and more lasting concerns will confer more meaning on the events that serve to fulfill or frustrate them. Outcomes pursued for their own sakes give meaning to instrumental actions and events leading up to them. One's deepest concerns, generating many other instrumental desires, typically relate to long-term projects and lasting personal relationships. Many such projects might serve to unite events into meaningful patterns: at the top careers and marriages, but also hobbies, travel, creative projects, athletic goals, friendships, and so on. Progress toward success generally sustains such projects, and ultimate success tends to confer lasting meaning to remembered pivotal events.

One's life appears to take on new meaning when one commits to new projects or relationships, focusing one's concerns, especially when these new projects integrate, reinterpret, or fulfill older concerns. Writing about meaning is presently meaningful to me because it continues my long-standing philosophical endeavors and fits my career plans. By contrast, a person suffers loss of meaning when he discovers that he was deceiving himself about motives or ends, when events do not seem to progress toward desired outcomes, when relationships break down or careers suffer serious setbacks. One then wonders what it was all for, whether one was all along pursuing meaningless goals, those that in the end fail to confer meaning on the activities in pursuit of them, or that lead to nothing further. If this manuscript fails to find a publisher, or (perish the thought) if I decide I was all wrong about meaning in life, my present activity will no longer seem so meaningful. (Doesn't that mean I wasn't wrong?)

Success

Success, then, matters. Pursuits that fail may seem pointless in retrospect, especially if there was little or no chance of succeeding to begin with. My trying to be a professional basketball player will not lead to a meaningful life for me no matter how long I persist in pursuing that impossible goal. In contrast, success brings a sense of fulfillment that heightens the meaning of the struggle to achieve it. And it relates the entire project to its external effects, giving it a meaning that failure lacks. If I am able to contribute significantly to the philosophical literature, then my philosophical pursuits have a meaning they would otherwise lack. They point beyond themselves to their results.

But success is not a necessary condition for activities to contribute to meaning in life, since it is the ongoing pursuit of goals and relationships that ties these activities together in intelligible structures. And we must remember that events can have negative as well as positive meaning. We saw that Macbeth's life was filled with such events. Even for us, unfortunately, a long-term project that ends in failure because of a single disastrous event will surely result in that event's having deep negative meaning.

Meaning here is tied not only to success as a facilitator, but to happiness as a common effect. The continuous achievement of our central concerns that lends meaning to the activities involved connects with happiness in so far as it contains the judgment that our lives are going well. Just as success and the feeling of fulfillment that accompanies it reflects meaning in the activities that led up to it, so it leads itself to happiness, other things being equal. Success breeds both meaning and happiness. But, as noted earlier, contentment with one's projects and relationships is again not sufficient for meaning. Along with others, we rejected Richard Taylor's claim that Sisyphus's accepting his lot and remaining content with his mindlessly repetitive task makes that activity meaningful. Nor is contentment necessary for meaning, since meaning can be negative as well as positive.

The narratively understood self is also closely associated with the long-term projects and relationships to which I have been referring. We are in one sense all that we have achieved personally and socially up to the present time. We define ourselves in terms of our relationships, careers, and other long-term pursuits that give meaning to our lives. I am a husband, father, philosopher, decent tennis player, golfer, and opera lover (you are at least a reader of philosophy). These are not just predicates that apply to me, but how I view myself and others view me. They express my central values, and pursuit of these values is again what confers meaning on events in my life. My central narratives relate to these most valued or important roles. I understand myself in terms of them, and fulfilling them successfully most saliently produces the meaning in my life.

Advice (?)

If I were asked to give advice on how to make life more meaningful, I would advise commitment to long-term projects and relationships. Challenging goals that require sustained pursuit through a variety of means provide more meaning in the long run, while short-lived satisfactions that come too easily seem shallow and relatively meaningless. Long-term commitment, if carried through, will make your life more meaningful, will make it seem more meaningful to you, but not necessarily better. I will have more to say in the final section about the connection or lack of connection between meaning and value. What I cannot do, and what no philosopher should attempt, is to give advice on how to make life better. There is only an unhelpful answer from the previous chapter: fulfill your deepest rational desires. This section is therefore the shortest in the book (but there are countless pop psychology alternatives).

Interpretations

Narratives are representations of meaningful events in people's lives. As representations they are both interpretations of the events and must themselves be interpreted. Meaning, in the sense in focus here, is, as noted, a three-term relation, the third term being the interpreter of the dyadic relation between the vehicle of meaning and its referent. Personal narratives that capture the meanings of events in lives are both the products of interpretations of events and interpreted by the subjects themselves.

Just as artworks and works of literature admit of different interpretations according to which the elements or episodes within them will have different meanings, so, as interpreters of our own lives, we can relate its events, and relate to them, in different ways. Trivially, events will take on different meanings for the optimist than for the pessimist, as they interpret them in different ways, as fulfillments of promises or threats or precursors of better or worse things to come. And different and incompatible ways of interpreting may be equally supported by the events themselves, which will have multiple and branching effects and causes. The birth of my first son meant learning for the first time the meaning of self-sacrifice, but also a new kind of love, a chance to relive my youth, the acquisition of responsibility such as I had not known before, and so on. All these were parts of different but related narratives in which the same event was interpreted differently.

I have noted that a person's life will admit of no single coherent narrative, but will have multiple narratives of different lengths and scopes, some fitting into others. And some events will enter into different narratives, where they will receive different interpretations. The births of my sons affected my career plans, marriage, moral commitments, value priorities, etc., and these events therefore had different meanings in these distinct narrative contexts. How I interpreted them was undoubtedly different from how my wife interpreted them, and I might have interpreted them differently also had I a different temperament.

Nature of interpretation

We interpret texts and events in order to understand them. We understand them by explaining them. Interpretations are a type of explanation. I have argued elsewhere that we interpret texts so as to maximize their value, in the case of literary texts their aesthetic or literary value, in the case of legal texts their social or moral value.[15] We explain how elements in the texts serve to enhance those values. Interpretations of events in our lives that give meaning to them by fitting them into personal narratives are also guided by our values, our personal value priorities. Their meanings will depend on how they affect the fulfillment or frustration of those values. The meaning of my son's birth to me depends partly on how it affects my career plans, limiting potential moves to areas with good schools, for example. This reflects the changing value priorities I assign to my position and his education.

Because people have different values and priorities among them, they will interpret the same events differently, assigning them different meanings in their different personal narratives. The same is true again of literary and legal interpretations, which may bring out different and often conflicting values (those which cannot be satisfied simultaneously)

---

[15] Goldman (2013), ch. 2; for a similar analysis, see also Dworkin (1986), ch. 2.

in the texts. There will therefore often be incompatible but equally acceptable interpretations warranted by the same texts or events. Scalia's momentous interpretation of the second amendment, taking reference to militias to be an unimportant illustration, was very different from the dissent that took it to be crucial in limiting individual rights to guns. Both could appeal to the same text, and the different interpretations reflected different value orientations, no matter how much each wanted to claim his interpretation to be value free. The interpretation of events is in this respect similar to the interpretation of texts.

I earlier described both a basic pre-narrative self or subject and a higher order narratively understood self that is constituted largely by the sum of personal narratives of past events implicitly grasped by the subject and projected in her future plans and projects. This higher order self expresses the subject's understanding of her character or relatively stable personality or behavioral dispositions. Relatively stable. But a person can not only act out of character, but can also reflect on and change, first her long-term plans and projects, and second even her dispositions and character, especially if she discovers that her earlier self-perceptions and understandings were largely self-deceptive. She will then reorient the ways she interprets past and possible future events in her life, assigning them new and different meanings and importance. Conflicts among personal values can also lead to such reassessments, as we saw in the example of assigning priority to universities or elementary schools in choosing a position (as if we had much choice). This is another source of variation in interpretive personal narratives.

Constraints

Despite acceptable variation, not just any way of interpreting is justified. We may to an extent give meaning to the events we experience, but we are constrained by their actual sequences, just as interpreters of literary, legal, or musical works are constrained by the texts or scores as written. Authors of fictional works are of course not so constrained by events, since they make up the events that enter their works as they go along. But the fictional events in their works as written do constrain the interpretations of their readers, just as in real life we often have little or no control over the events that affect our lives. Events need not be intended in order to have great effect and meaning in our lives. Objective occurrences of events beyond our control, and even intentional actions once performed and choices once made, constrain our interpretations or personal narratives, just as texts as written constrain their acceptable interpretations. We select events in memory for relevance to our narratives, but some will be salient whether we like it or not. This is especially true of negatively valued events, whether we are overwhelmed or able to overcome them.

We are also constrained in our lives and in the construction of our personal narratives by the social roles that our cultures and our backgrounds make available to us. We do not invent careers, but choose among those accessible to us. Relationships are also somewhat constrained by what is socially acceptable and available at a time, and by whom we happen to meet by chance. Careers are not fated for us in the way that God's plan was traditionally thought to determine the course of our lives, and we might pursue them in unique ways, but they are still socially contoured. And actions within these social roles fall into somewhat predictable and familiar patterns and narratives.

We choose how to pursue our projects and relationships, but we choose only among those that society and chance present to us. In this way also, what is objectively given constrains the meanings we can ascribe to the events that make up the narratives of our lives. Finally, these narratives themselves must be socially confirmed to be normally sustained. It is difficult without elaborate psychological mechanisms not to see ourselves as others see us. The personal narratives of normal people must receive confirmation in the perceptions of others. In all these ways meanings in our lives are as much given to us as determined through our interpretations. I might try to interpret myself as a philosophical genius, but that would be hard to maintain while still awaiting social confirmation. Only Donald Trump types are capable of sustaining inflated self-images in the face of any and all counterevidence.

That personal narratives are both objectively constrained and open to interpretation implies an answer to another question that will arise regarding the meaning of events in our lives: a person can be mistaken in regard to the meanings he ascribes. The real life Trump example evidences this. We noted earlier that Macbeth was mistaken about the meaning of events in his life. (His being fictional is no impediment to what we can learn from him.) Their sequence appeared to him incoherent, lacking in any intelligible patterns, when in fact the various central events in the play—the witches' prophesies, the murders of Duncan and Banquo, and so on—led inevitably to his ultimate demise. These events all had negative meaning, but meaning nevertheless. That he could not appreciate their meaning meant that his life was meaningless to him, however meaningful his life, his motives, and the events that ensued from them are to others, including primarily the readers of the play. While Macbeth mistook the meanings of events in his life even in retrospect (he did not have time to reflect on them, the quoted speech having been made in the face of death on the battlefield), more commonly when events lead to unexpected outcomes, a person will mistake their meaning at the time of their occurrence. I took the chance meeting of my future wife to mean only a potentially amusing date; only much later did it take on momentous significance in my life. An opposite sort of change or correction in meaning occurs when one decides that what she was pursuing is not worth the effort, in which case earlier efforts might lose their meaning for her.

A person's self-image is based only on her own interpretation of meaningful events in her life. But once more her own personal narratives are vulnerable to disconfirmation by others with whom she interacts. Character, if real, is narratively understood but not narratively constructed. I am not taking a firm stand here on the situationists' claim that circumstances far more than character determine actions. It suffices to say that we assume the reality of character when we predict actions in situations in which we know that different individuals will act differently. And, without any hard evidence, it seems we are pretty good at it when we know the individuals in question well. Once more, a person can be self-deceptive, mistaken about his own character, which again assumes there is something to be mistaken about.

However that may be, the main points of this section have been that we interpret events in our lives in assigning them meanings in our personal narratives, that these interpretations are constrained by objective occurrences and social norms, that they can be mistaken and are vulnerable to disconfirmation and subject to revision, but that meaning in life from the first person perspective at a given time depends only on one's own interpretation of past events as possibly projected into future plans and decisions.

The Value of Meaning in Life

I have described the nature of meaning in life; now we may ask about its value. In earlier chapters I characterized both pleasure and happiness as partial constituents of personal value, what is valuable to individuals themselves, and I also provided an account of well-being, the all-inclusive category equivalent to personal value. Like pleasure and happiness, meaning in life is a partial constituent of well-being, although in its case there is more variation in its personal value. The ascetic who eschews pleasure is a rarer bird, more out of line with the other ducks, than the individual who lives for the moment and cares little about coherence over time in his life. Nevertheless, the connection between meaning in life, as coherent patterns of events within one's life, and well-being, as the satisfaction of rational desires, is quite close for most of us.

Individual differences

Most of us desire coherence in our lives. We pursue long-term career achievements instead of flitting from one career or job to another, and we marry and have children, presumed lifelong personal commitments in relationships. Fulfillment in these projects and relationships gives meaning to our lives, and most of us seek such fulfillment. There are more superficial signs of the quest for coherence in our lives as well. We seek out reminders of our pasts and their links to the present: we go to reunions and log into Facebook, where we renew old friendships; we keep photo albums and mementos that keep the meanings of old events alive;[16] and we tell personal stories to our friends and acquaintances about our past achievements and foibles (however true or false they might be).

Not everyone, though, cares about such meanings from their past lives. Meaning in life, like all other things, matters only to those who care about it. If all value for us derives ultimately from our concerns or from what we care about, as I argued in the previous chapter, this will be true also of the value for us of meaning in our lives. And this value will differ depending on how much we care about it. Perhaps most people prefer challenge, complexity, diversity, and long range projects in their lives that lend to them cumulative progression and narrative intelligibility. But others might prefer the more relaxed and comfortable routine of repetition or the excitement of living in the moment. Eventually many might reach a point where the quest for new meanings itself seems pointless, and there is nothing wrong with looking forward to retirement on the golf course (as reflected in my aforementioned desire to finish this book).

---

[16] A similar point is made by Schecterman (2007).

But everyone seeks to pursue the ends they set for themselves, to pursue whatever they value in life, even if only lower golf scores, and such pursuit lends meaning to events as it progresses, even if not for the long term (we have seen that not all such meaning is positive; for the unfortunate, most events have negative meaning). Everyone wants to achieve future ends, however seemingly trivial, although not everyone cares, or cares equally, about past achievements. So meaning itself is more fleeting for some than for others, although perhaps never completely absent as we continually interpret what is happening around us and relate it to our concerns, however momentary or long-term. Meaning in life is, as noted before, a matter of degree, and once more judging it involves the assumption of a comparison class. Both the person who leads a life of dull repetition and the one who flits from one superficial concern to another are still leading relatively meaningless lives.

For all people, the meanings they find in events are relative to what they value, to how those events affect what they value. Agents pursue projects that reflect their own values, and meaning derives from the way that pursuit of these concerns connects various activities and events into intelligible narratives. Positively valuable projects and relationships are more easily sustainable than heinous projects and exploitative relationships, although value here is given an internal or subjective instead of external or objective interpretation (more on that below). Again, not all valuable activities have great meaning for the individuals engaged in them, only those that relate diverse events over time. Helping an old person across the street, writing a check to a charity, or seeing a beautiful flower or bird may not confer much meaning unless part of a broader plan, however good these actions or experiences might be.[17] Moral value, aesthetic value, as well as other kinds, do not equate in themselves with meaning. But not only are valued projects and relationships more easily sustained, valued events are more easily remembered and incorporated into meaning-conferring narratives.

Even those of us normal people who care greatly about coherence and meaning in our lives do not place that concern above all other values. The meaningfulness of a life is only one aspect relevant to its evaluation, and its value for the person leading the life may have to be balanced

---

[17] Wolf (1997) makes the same point about charity, although she does not mention broader plans.

against other values. Meaning in life is not only distinct from happiness and pleasure, but might come into conflict with them. Too much coherence would be for most of us a bad thing. The most coherent life is one spent in pursuit of a single cause to which all else is subordinate. That is the life of a fanatic. The rest of us seek diversity as well as coherence and extended meaning. And given the vicissitudes of life, if we try to make our lengthier narratives perfectly coherent, we will most often falsify them. Only fictional narratives can be perfectly coherent.

The context of the question

On a personal level, the question of meaning in life usually arises only when one begins to lose a grip on meanings formerly taken for granted. Meaning is called into question when projects seem to lose their point, become simply repetitive, or seem to be going nowhere. Projects confer meaning, but then we can ask for the meaning of the projects. Eventually, if we are questioning only meaning, these questions themselves become meaningless, like the questions of a child who keeps asking why, no matter what the previous answer was. But questioning the value of a project when we are not sure whether we continue to value or care about it always makes sense. This is another link between meaning and value. When we begin to ask whether what we are doing is really worthwhile, whether it has any value, whether we really care about it anymore, that is when we question as well the meanings that our projects confer. When we no longer care about a goal or end, the means we have been using to achieve it lose their meaning. Do I really want to write a ninth book, hoping it will bring me the fame that the other eight have not (partially fictional example)? Loss of meaning often results from loss of value.

This happens, however, only when we reflectively come to question our freely chosen projects and relationships, when we have time to become spectators of our lives. Meeting necessities does not raise questions of meaning. One might question whether a marriage continues to confer meaning on her life, but not whether her children do so when she must provide for them. From the first person perspective, we question our narratives and their meanings when we reflect on the course of our lives and ask ourselves whether we should change them. From the third person perspective, we question the narratives we ascribe to others when they seem to act out of character, unexpectedly. We then ask whether they really have the values we thought they had, whether things mean to them what we thought they meant. Questions of value and meaning tend to arise simultaneously when we are taken aback and react with reflection.

Objective Value

The value I have been linking with meaning is not the objective value that Susan Wolf and others think must be referenced in an account of meaning in life. As noted at the beginning of this chapter, they think that projects and commitments must be objectively valuable in order to provide meaning in life. Wolf writes:

> The idea of meaning is the idea of doing something you're subjectively very attracted to, engaged by, excited by, but the thing to which you're devoting all this energy and attention is also objectively valuable.[18]

She believes that appeal to objective value is required here because subjective commitment to a project is not sufficient for it to confer meaning on life. I agreed earlier that Sisyphus's being committed to rolling the stone does not suffice for his life of doing only that to be meaningful. A life of watching TV soaps or sports is not meaningful no matter how committed to such activities a person is, no matter how much pleasure or happiness he finds in them. Wolf reasons that if subjective commitment is not sufficient, there must be an objective condition as well that is necessary for meaning in life, and the obvious candidate is that one's projects and relationships must have objective value.

The concept

The first problem with her view is her admission that she has no account of objective value, only intuitions about which activities have it and which don't:

> I don't have a theory of objective value in which everything with objective value has property X... I'm starting from our communal intuitions about what's valuable and what's not.[19]

Unfortunately, I am not a member of her community as far as some of these intuitions go, and I suspect that many others are not either. As with other objectivists, her intuitions seem to reflect only her own subjective values or preferences. According to her, the lives of corporate

---

[18] Wolf (2014), pp. 267–8.   [19] Wolf (2014), p. 268.

lawyers and pig farmers lack meaning, while presumably those of labor lawyers and epistemologists (whom others might accuse of playing glass beads games) do not. Farmers and business executives would judge very differently, even if they accepted her notions of objective value and meaningfulness. For her, doing philosophy is objectively valuable and therefore meaningful, but solving Sudoku puzzles is not. Being an Olympic athlete is valuable and therefore meaningful, and so is writing poetry, even if it is never published and no one reads it.[20]

Can we make sense of any of this (aside from the preferences of a liberal, white, female philosopher)? One might think that a distinction in value between philosophy and Sudoku lies in the fact that others benefit from reading the philosophy one writes, but no one benefits from the solutions to the Sudoku puzzles. But then she allows the poetry to be valuable and meaningful even when no one reads it. Being an Olympic athlete is valuable, she suggests, because it involves doing something very well, exercising the virtue of discipline, and being part of a community. But then solving Sudoku puzzles meets these criteria too, if one is part of a puzzle solving community. Yet presumably she would still find it a meaningless if pleasurable activity. As for philosophers versus corporate lawyers and farmers, not only the lawyers and farmers, but corporate heads and bacon lovers would disagree in regard to their value. Are her distinctions anything more than slightly disguised narrow-mindedness? She also admits activities that are (objectively) valuable but do not confer meaning, such as writing checks to charity. Her explanation for their lack of meaning is that they do not provide a sense of fulfillment. But why not, and for that matter, can't the solution to a Sudoku puzzle provide that sense?

I agree with at least some of her intuitions about meaningful activities (having two corporate lawyer sons, not that one!), those regarding checks to charity and Sudoku puzzles,[21] but I offer a different explanation. The former is presumably an isolated activity, and the latter is more or less repetitive, while I have located meaning in the relation of activities or events to others in developing narratives. Once more, if the act of charity is part of an ongoing pattern of different charitable activities, or if it is

---

[20] Wolf (2014), pp. 268, 270–1.

[21] I agree with her about Sudoku. A referee for this manuscript did not—another indication that we are talking about subjects valuing things and nothing more.

known to have a profound effect in itself on the lives of others, it will acquire a meaning that it otherwise would lack. And if, for example, the solution to the Sudoku puzzle wins a contest that results in a trip to Japan for further competition, then it too will become meaningful.

Relation to meaning and action

Without an account of objective value, and with seemingly conflicting intuitions as to when such value confers meaning, the appeal to this concept first of all appears empty. The second problem with the appeal to objective value as the condition added to subjective commitment as the key to meaning is, as noted at the beginning of this chapter, that it has nothing to do with meaning in any ordinary sense. Instead of providing an account of meaning, it simply changes the subject. This dual appeal to commitment and objective value as necessary and sufficient for meaning is the dominant view at present, held by other prominent philosophers as well as Susan Wolf, but, like her, no writer on meaning has provided either a satisfactory account of objective value itself, or of why it has anything to do with meaning as ordinarily understood. I argued earlier that a valuable life is not necessarily a meaningful life. Almost everyone's life is important or valuable to them. As for value to others, a person who accidentally and unwittingly discovers a cure for cancer, without preparing for or following up on it, and whose discovery is recognized as such only after her death, will have led a very valuable life but not necessarily a meaningful one.

Third, in the earlier chapters I noted problems for the very concept of objective value. First, from the perspective of practical reasoning, it is superfluous. This can be put in the form of a dilemma. On the one hand, objective value need have no connection with any of our current concerns or motivations. That is just what "objective" means— independence from our subjective states. But if there were no such connection, there could be no practical relevance to the existence of such value. How could the world demand that all our concerns be other than they are? Could you accept a demand to not care for yourself or your loved ones and to pursue some conflicting values instead? An objectivist will say that caring for loved ones is objectively valuable, but surely that is not the source of our motivation to do so. Our loved ones might be relatively worthless, but we still care for them.

How could we recognize objective value? We can judge what is valuable only from the perspective of what we value or find valuable.[22] Completely alien values would remain just that whether objective or not. It would be utterly mysterious how such an alien value could require or prompt motivation from us. Why would this value give us any reason to pursue it if it relates to none of our concerns? The only answer could be that we would be better off if we had such a concern. But how could we be better off if none of our informed concerns were better satisfied? Of course a value that is at first personally alien could become part of one's motivational set if highly valued by a person one cares deeply about. As Aristotle noted, true friendship involves pursuing the welfare of one's friend, and therefore valuing what she values. Value can be transmitted in that way, but then it does become connected to one's own concerns. Objective value that is unconnected remains practically inert. Playing the harmonica might be held to have objective value, but I see no reason for me to do it.

It is open to the objectivist to argue that objective values must be subjectively valued in order to be relevant to our practical decisions. But if objective values matched our own values or concerns, the appeal to them would again be superfluous from a practical perspective. If we already care about what has objective value, then we are motivated to pursue it whether or not its value is objective. We do not care about things because we want our values to be objective; instead, things seem to have or lack value because we care about or value them, or, as Wolf views corporate law, we don't value them. We don't love others because we think they are objectively worth loving. We love people whom others don't love, and similarly, what is a valuable project for us is not for others. Yogi Berra said that he would rather be the Yankee's catcher than president;[23] Hilary Clinton would not agree with that value priority.

The objectivist can say that choice of which values to pursue is just that—optional choice. But claiming that pursuit of objective value is optional is itself problematic. If it is better that we pursue objective rather than merely subjective values, isn't it better that we pursue greater rather than lesser objective value? Then how is such choice optional? Our focus

---

[22] This point has been emphasized by Harry Frankfurt in many writings. See, for example, Frankfurt (2004).

[23] He said many other wonderful things. See Goldman (2009) for a large sample.

on the objects of our concerns and not on our desires themselves makes the value of those objects seem objective. But, as in the case of colors and other secondary qualities, the phenomenology can be metaphysically misleading.

Wolf would reply again that being concerned, committed, or "actively engaged" in various pursuits is not sufficient for making them meaningful, and that their having objective worth must be the additional necessary condition that, together with commitment, is necessary for meaningfulness. But my criterion of meaningfulness is independent of subjective commitment, although I have noted that being committed to a project sustains it and facilitates its narrative expression in memory. The point here is that just as appeal to objective value is superfluous in practical reasoning, it is so as well in regard to meaning. If we value our long-term projects and relationships, then the events that constitute and influence them will have meaning for us. And if they lose their value for us, then whatever meaning they conferred on events will quickly fade or turn negative. The objectivity of the value, or lack of it, has nothing to do with this relation between meaning and value.

Other arguments against objective value from the previous chapters, such as the lack of apparent unity in the objects that are supposed to have it (other than being objects of desire or concern), and the lack of any conception of how to maximize it, need not be repeated here. It is worth noting here that just as this concept replaces appeal to a supernatural being generally in contemporary philosophy, so objective value plays the traditional role of God's plan in contemporary philosophers' discussions of meaningful lives. Its pursuit is supposed to give our lives meaning or purpose without our having to create such purpose or interpret such meaning. It provides an external standard for our subjective values and pursuits to meet, validating the ways we value things (everyone thinks her own values objective) and providing reasons for the motivations we have and meanings we find. Like God's plan, it provides ready-made external meaning that we have only to recognize and commit to.

But we have seen that just as God's plan would not create meaning in our lives unless we understood, accepted, and made this our plan or purpose for us, so objective value would remain irrelevant to our lives unless it connected to our concerns or motivations. For those philosophers for whom objective value plays the role of God's plan in providing an external framework for meaning in life, an admission that all value is subjective would again make the question of meaning pressing. But I have argued that the question can be answered within the subjectivist framework in terms of projects and relationships that we value, conferring meaning on events in our lives.

We have also seen that the external world, both social and physical, independent of our concerns does have a role to play in initiating and sustaining our meaning-conferring projects and relationships. The social world provides roles that largely frame our projects and relationships, and the world at large must allow these projects to proceed to fulfillment. The objective world independent of us provides many of the things we value (for which there is an evolutionary explanation), and it allows us to produce many other things of value. Its sustaining or frustrating our values is the ubiquitous effect of luck in our lives, along with the smart or stupid choices we make in response to it. But the values we find in it are our values, and we need appeal to no others in order to explain the meanings we find in events in our lives.

Summary

I have argued that, in the absence of any known grand eschatological narrative into which our lives jointly fit and which gives them common purpose and meaning, we can still find meaning in our lives in the meaningful events that fill them. This is a commonly ascribed type of meaning, unlike what is characterized as meaning in life in other contemporary philosophical accounts, primarily commitment to objectively valuable activities. Events in our lives acquire meaning by relating to each other in coherent narratives. Not all people equally value such coherence in their lives, and those who do value it, if they are not fanatically committed to a single cause, do not aspire to the kind of near perfect coherence found in the best fictional literature. But as rationally desired by many or most, meaning in life is, like pleasure and happiness, a significant part of well-being. I hope to have shown that pleasure, happiness, and meaning are all typical sources or components of well-being, but only because they are rationally desired by us, given the way we are.

Conclusions

I have both distinguished and related pleasure, happiness, well-being, and meaning. I have related each to motivation and value. In regard to pleasure, I distinguished three irreducible kinds, relating each to its opposite in pain, and to motivation and value. I claimed that regarding happiness as primarily an emotion captured what earlier accounts in terms of judgments or feelings got right. The emotion was contrasted with two higher order related states of happiness: moods and temperaments. Once more the limited place of happiness in motivation and value was explained. I claimed that well-being, the all-inclusive category of personal value, consists in the known satisfaction of central rational desires. The value of the other states then depends on the degree to which they are rationally desired, and this will vary among individuals. This account of well-being was contrasted with hedonist, perfectionist, and objective list accounts. In the appendix, I analyze desire as a cluster concept, similar to emotion, and contrast this account with a contemporary neurophysical reductionist account.

Now grasping all these relations among these desirable states, please draw your own conclusions. Pursue your own rational desires, as you will, without regretting that I could not tell you how to live. Now you will have to find your pleasure, happiness, well-being, and meaning elsewhere than in this book, which I hope gave you a bit of each. May your future pleasures be many, your happiness often experienced, your well-being great, and your meaning whatever you make of it.

Desires

I have defined well-being in terms of the satisfaction of central rational desires. I have not offered an analysis of desire itself. This appendix will remedy that omission. The analysis I will offer parallels the account of emotions in the second chapter, Happiness. Desires and emotions are structurally similar states with different but related motivational functions.

Review of Criteria

Let us first recall the ground rules: the criteria for an acceptable account of a psychological state. Remember that the first is that it must capture our ordinary concept. An account would simply change the subject if it bore little relation to the term or concept of desire as we use and apply it. There would be no point in calling an analysis that failed this test an account of desire. Such an account must fit our linguistic intuitions as to when we should ascribe a desire to a person and the reasons we offer for doing so. The second criterion involves capturing relations to similar states, here the functionally related states of desires and emotions.

The third ground refers to the relation of the state to motivation. Since desires themselves are motivational states including behavioral dispositions, we are here referring to explanations and predictions of behavior by appeal to desires. The context in which we predict behavior on the basis of ascribed desires is that of everyday social interaction. In that context the folk psychological concept of desire that I will describe has great predictive power and helps to explain our widespread success in interacting as successfully as we do. The main competing account is the reductionist theory that identifies desire with a state of the brain. I point out initially that finding the neurological underpinnings of desire may be useful for diagnosing disorders relating to desires, motivation, and behavior, but it has no use in ordinary contexts of social interaction.

The grounds for assessing competing accounts of desire should fit nicely together if the concept as currently used and applied figures prominently in explanations and predictions of behavior. Both the account I will advocate and the one I will criticize claim to satisfy all these grounds together. Another question is how well a folk psychological account of desire must fit the current state of neuroscience or its more mature successor. If the latter is to reduce our ordinary concept instead of eliminating it, the requirement runs the other way. I will argue below that a neat mapping onto a single brain structure is not necessary to the preservation of the folk psychological category.

My Account

The cluster concept

The analysis of desire I advocate sees the term as referring, as does the previously defended analysis of emotion, to a cluster concept. It will be well to recall the contours of such concepts at the start. A cluster concept does not have individually sufficient conditions for its application. It has multiple criteria. When all are present, they are sufficient for counting the object as a paradigm of its kind. Fewer may be sufficient for including the object within the category, but such an object will not be a paradigm. There might be disagreement about whether to include it in the category, and a subconcept might apply, for example a wish instead of a full-fledged desire. As noted in an earlier reference to desires, they can take only future objects. If the Dolphins have already lost the game, I do not say, "I desire that they had won," but I do say, "I wish that they had won."

Some properties may be necessary for an object's being of the kind in question—desires are necessarily mental states—but these properties define only the broader class that contains the kind. The criterial properties are not mere contingent effects of the states, but constitutive of them, but this does not prevent them from causally interacting. Recall in the case of emotions that a person can tremble and flee because she is afraid, but the disposition to tremble and flee are definitive of what it is to be afraid and not mere contingent effects of fear.

We determine which properties belong in a given cluster by noting the usage of the term or concept. On what bases do all English speakers agree that someone desires something (especially when he does not simply say that he desires it)? When people disagree, what reasons do they give for ascribing or withholding ascription of a desire? And finally, on what more specific grounds do they predict behavior by appealing to desires?

According to my analysis, prototypical instances of desire then have all of the criterial cluster of properties, while less clear instances have some but not all of the properties in the cluster. Thus, to take a simple paradigm, my desire to play golf disposes me to find courses and tee times, directs my attention to ads for affordable green fees, produces pleasant thoughts of long drives and sunk putts, involves the evaluative judgment that the exercise and relaxation would be good for me, and, especially when faced with a pile of ungraded student tests, produces a certain yearning sensation akin to an urge. It may also produce other desires, say for a new putter.

A paradigm desire for x thus disposes one to bring about x, produces pleasant thoughts of x, involves a positive evaluative judgment of x, a yearning sensation in its absence, a direction of attention to things related to x, and possibly produces other instrumental desires for means to satisfy it. Most of these elements—affective, cognitive, and conative—are first-person introspectable. When we ascribe desires to others, and in so doing possibly predict their behavior, we again do so by how they say they feel, how they evaluate various objects, what they pay attention to and take pleasure in, and what their behaviors seem to aim at. We again judge dispositional, attentional, sensational, representational, and evaluative factors.

In regard to nonparadigm cases, none of these facets of the paradigms are necessary or sufficient for ascribing desire. In regard to necessity, instrumental desires such as my desire for a dentist appointment lack pleasant thoughts; long-standing desires might not direct attention until opportunities arise for satisfying them; my wish for good weather will not dispose me to do anything about it and might lack a yearning sensation; and addictive desires might lack positive evaluative judgments. In regard to sufficiency, I can be disposed to act out of habit, not desire; I can feel an urge, say violent or sexual, without being disposed to fulfill it, and then it is not clear that it is a full-fledged desire; I can judge certain things like kale to be good for me without desiring them; and I can have pleasant thoughts about the past or about fantasy worlds without desiring to bring them about. Thus we define the concept of desire not by stating necessary and sufficient conditions, but precisely in terms of the criterial properties of paradigms.

While none of the properties of prototypical desires is singly necessary or sufficient, a number of them occurring together can suffice for ascribing desire. Furthermore, they normally interact to causally influence or reinforce one another. As in the case of emotions, some of the criterial states can cause others to occur. A positive evaluative judgment, for example, can produce pleasant thoughts or a disposition to pursue its object. The cluster analysis characterizes the concept of desire as a functional concept since the properties or states in the cluster intervene between sensory inputs and behavioral outputs, but the criterial effects are variable.

The primary function of desire is dispositional or motivational—desire is a state that prototypically aims to bring about its own satisfaction—and so the dispositional element of the cluster is central, but while this element is the state of being motivated, other elements exert motivational force. As indicated above, not even the dispositional factor is necessary in ascribing desire—I can want there to be good weather tomorrow without being disposed to do anything about it—but the centrality of this factor is indicated by the fact that we then tend to use different terms: I hope or wish for good weather, while "I desire good weather" is somewhat unnatural.

The Reductionist Account

Rewards

In their recent book, *In Praise of Desire*, Nomy Arpaly and Timothy Schroeder offer a very different account (essentially the same account proposed by Schroeder in his earlier book, *Three Faces of Desire*). According to them, while some of the effects listed above in the cluster may indicate how we identify desires, they are just that: *contingent effects* of desires. On my account some of the criterial properties can cause others, but together they constitute desires instead of being effects of desires. On their account desire itself is what in the brain contingently causes these effects (or at least some of them). And what in the brain causes these effects is the operation of the reward system, the system that is responsible for reward-based learning.

Thus, for them, to have the desire that p is to constitute the representation of p as a reward.[1] A reward figures in reward-based learning by increasing the disposition of one mental state to cause another[2] and ultimately to cause a certain type of behavior. The system releases a positive learning signal (in the form of dopamine) when a certain representation (reward) occurs.[3] We thereby come to think and act in ways likely to lead to rewards. The release of this signal therefore typically causes the effects associated with desires: pleasurable feelings and dispositions to behave in certain ways. But although we refer to these effects in identifying the reward system, they do not define the system. To desire that p is to respond to the representation that p so as to increase the chance of a positive reward learning signal being released, although this chance is discounted to the degree to which the satisfaction of the desire is expected. (So too then is the feeling of pleasure, pleasure being seen as the representation of change in desire satisfaction relative to expectation.)

The alleged advantages of this theory derive from the fact that desire is characterized here as a natural kind that contingently causes the typical effects by which it is typically identified. An analogy is drawn by Arpaly and Schroeder to the natural kind water and a contrast to air. We identify water in everyday contexts by its effects on us: its color, odor, taste (or lack of same), capacity for quenching thirst, etc. And these means of identification might exhaust the concept of the scientifically naïve. But water is H_2O. Its typical effects are not constitutive of what water is. It might cause different effects in different possible worlds, but it would still be water, what causes these effects in us. Similarly, for Arpaly and Schroeder desires are what cause typical effects in us, which effects do not constitute its nature. In us those effects are caused by states of the reward system. If the analogy to water is sound, these states must be defined in structural or material terms, not functional or causal terms, although, like water, they can be identified in our world by their typical effects.

By contrast, air is not a natural kind because there is no single cause of the various ways we identify air, for example as what blows, as what we breathe, etc. It is nitrogen that mostly accounts for wind, and oxygen that

---

[1] Arpaly and Schroeder (2014), p. 127.
[2] Arpaly and Schroeder (2014), p.129.
[3] I will not question the neurophysiology here. It has been questioned by Katz (2005).

allows us to breathe. It is because the operation of the reward system is the single (contingent) cause of the typical effects by which we identify desire that we can construe desiring, identified with this operation, as a natural kind. It is implied that if these effects were caused by a disjunction of neural states, desire would not be a natural kind. In fact, it might not appear as a term in mature science.

If we are to identify desire with a state of the brain, present neurological evidence suggests that the operation of the reward system is that state. Arpaly and Schroeder argue that it is the only thing that causes what desires cause.[4] Furthermore, it is a discrete physical system in the brain that operates by releasing a certain chemical, dopamine. Both these features are crucial to the plausibility of the account to scientifically minded philosophers. In the absence of a natural kind or discrete system in the brain that has the effects we associate with desires, the concept of desire would not figure in the causal explanations of mature physical science: it would be eliminated instead of reduced. But then we would lack an explanation for the degree to which our present folk concept of desire allows for predictions and explanations of behavior. It is because the reward system in itself causes what desires cause that we can identify its states or operations with the presence of desires. And, once more, it is only those states that cause what desires cause, so that this is the only candidate for the reduction at which physicalists aim.

Arpaly and Schroeder, following Hume, claim that illuminating causal explanations must refer to only contingent causal relations. Unlike the criterial cluster account, in which desires are constituted by their motivational factors, the reductive account according to them can explain these phenomena by appealing to desires, giving it greater explanatory power. If informative causal explanations must refer to only contingent causal relations, then their account will indeed have greater explanatory power than the cluster analysis of desire. And explanatory power is a major criterion for ranking theories. But, as noted earlier, I deny the premise.

Natural Kinds and Functions

Arpaly and Schroeder characterize desire as a functional or psychological natural kind because it is defined as what causes certain typical mental

---

[4] Arpaly and Schroeder (2014), p. 142.

and behavioral effects.[5] The reward system could be implemented differently, that is, in different physical realizations. Perhaps in other creatures other chemicals might play the role of dopamine. But, as emphasized, Arpaly and Schroeder see the causal relations of the reward system to its effects to be always contingent. I want to question whether what they see as effects of desire, namely motivation and pleasure, are correctly seen as contingent effects. I have included other facets of desire along with these two and have admitted that none is necessary or sufficient. But the cluster analysis does not equate lack of necessity and sufficiency with mere contingency. The relation of the elements of the cluster to desire itself (as with any other cluster concept) is criterial, not merely contingent. The contrast becomes clearer when we examine more closely their opposing notion of a natural psychological kind.

They explain their position mainly through the analogy to water.[6] But this analogy to water as a physical natural kind is imperfect at best and misleading at worst. H_2O is water in all possible worlds, whatever its effects in other worlds on us or alien creatures. The ultimate test is simply chemical composition. We folk understand that water is a chemical compound, and even the most scientifically naïve among us grasp that it is a physical substance of some kind. Thus, even though we identify it in everyday contexts by its observable features and effects, it is not best construed as a functional concept at all. Or, if we are to force the concept into the functional mold, it must be construed as a realizer concept and not as a role concept. That is, water is whatever physical substance causes its effects in us, the same physical substance in possible worlds without those effects. What is definitive is not the causal role it plays in our or any world, but the physical substance that contingently realizes that role here.

The reward system is a physical system in the brain responsible for releasing dopamine at certain times. But we cannot plausibly think of desire as a physical or physiological kind. A structurally identical physical state in the head of a Martian that has none of the mental properties that we associate with desires, that does not affect motivation, attention, pleasant thoughts, or evaluative judgments, would not provide us with any temptation to conceptualize it as desire. What desires in us and

---

[5] Arpaly and Schroeder (2014), pp. 162, 177.
[6] Arpaly and Schroeder (2014), p. 177.

in alien beings have in common is not some physical state of brains, but precisely the properties that we think of as being in the cluster described above.

The whole point of thinking of desire as a functional state is to recognize its multiple realizability in physical terms. As noted, for Arpaly and Schroeder the reward system is a psychological kind that might be multiply physically realized, although they seem to think it crucial that there is a single or discrete physical realization. But if that system is only contingently related to its effects, the concept of desire that equates it with a state of the reward system must again be what is called a realizer concept. By contrast, if the cluster properties are criterial, the functional concept of desire must be a role functional concept.[7] That is, the properties of the cluster that are seen by them as its effects cannot be eliminated from its analysis.

The functional analysis of desire must be more like a functional analysis of color concepts than like the concept of a physical substance like water. We cannot identify the color red simply with the light waves that appear red to us, since if they appeared otherwise they would not fall under our current concept of red. If things that appear red to us appeared the same way as blue things do, so that we could not distinguish things in the present two classes on the basis of color, we would not apply our present concept of red to them. In fact, that concept would disappear. The way of appearing, an observable property as red is, is essential to an object's being red. Similarly, the properties of our cluster that the functionalist sees as mere effects of desires cannot be only contingently related to desires proper. They are again the only properties that we conceive of all and only paradigm desires having in common.

But then, should we think of desire as a functional or essentially causal concept at all? In one sense yes, since, as mentioned, the cluster properties themselves intervene between inputs and outputs and motivate or cause behavioral effects. But need we view them as simply effects of a hidden physical cause that is the real desire? When we observe other persons or see ourselves as having all the properties of the cluster, we immediately know that they or we are in the grip of a desire. We do not need to infer a hidden cause of the motivational state in the brain,

---

[7] See, for example, Cohen (2005).

whether single, as reductionists seem to think necessary, or multiple and disjunctive. If we want to know whether a particular person desires a particular outcome and want to predict her behavior on that basis, we ask whether she expresses pleasant thoughts about it, whether she directs attention to it in her plans, whether she evaluates it as good, and so on.

It is worth noting also that the central function of the reward system, producing a certain type of automatic learning through reinforcement, is not what we think of as the central function of desire, that is, together with beliefs directly motivating action to satisfy it. Desire aims at satisfaction as belief aims at truth: these are constitutive aims, defining the states to be the kinds they are. What satisfies a desire constitutes its content and defines it to be the desire it is. The reward system produces motivation as discounted by expectation, but is not itself a motivational state. It has a function: to produce or strengthen the disposition or motivational state. The behavioral disposition as the central part of the cluster is that motivational state, while pleasant thoughts and evaluative judgments motivate, and directed attention is a means to fulfill the motivation.

Being in the grip of a desire just is, it seems, being motivated or disposed to certain courses of action, having pleasant thoughts of the object not yet possessed, judging it good to obtain it, etc. An analysis that sees these as only contingent effects loses what is common to desires across possible worlds. The cluster with different physical causes still seems to constitute desires, while the reward system, if it could have different effects, which it could if they are only contingent, does not. In his earlier book Schroeder explicitly bites the bullet and claims that a creature with no dispositions to behave and no feelings could still have desires.[8] He briefly repeats that claim in the later book.[9] But that bullet will break your teeth.

Sufficiency

According to my account, none of the criterial conditions for desire are necessary or sufficient. According to the reductionist account, the operation of the reward system is sufficient.[10] So it is worth pointing out that

---

[8] Schroeder (2004), p. 138.   [9] Arpaly and Schroeder (2014), p. 114.
[10] Other philosophers also focus on only one aspect of desire as sufficient. Thus Joseph Raz (1999) and Thomas Scanlon (1998) emphasize the cognitive aspect. Ruth Chang (2004)

it is not. Reward is not sufficient for desire because we can try something entirely new and unanticipated and find it highly rewarding, acquiring the disposition to seek it again. If unanticipated, it was not desired but still constituted as a reward when acquired. Arpaly and Schroeder hold that one can desire what one already possesses,[11] and so they can reply to this case that the unexpected object is both constituted as a reward *and* desired once it is experienced for the first time. But first, this reply flies in the face of all traditional descriptions of the phenomenology of desire at least as far back as those of Hobbes, Descartes, and Hume.[12] As noted earlier, these descriptions are also supported by ordinary language observations. I would not say that I want the Dolphins to win when I know that they just did win. Nor would I say that I want the cake that I am eating.

The centrality of the motivational element in full-fledged desire, as opposed to mere wish, which can refer to the past or present, also supports the intuition that all such desire is for some future state of affairs. We can certainly desire that some present pleasurable state of affairs continue or repeat, but that is a desire for the future. And especially in the case of a pleasant surprise, fleetingness may be part of its charm, so that a desire for continuation might well be absent (as also with an unexpectedly satisfying meal).

One could also reply to the lack of sufficiency in the reward system in such examples by positing a standing desire for various pleasurable experiences. This would imply the existence of a desire before the attainment of the reward. But first, it would be the wrong desire, since the pleasure is a byproduct of the attainment of the object initially constituted as a reward. Second, this would trivialize the account by an ad hoc move, since one could then posit a desire for anything that pleases or turns out to please. Rewards would always mark satisfaction of desire

and G. F. Schueler (1995) focus on the affective aspect. Alfred Mele (2003) and Elijah Millgram (1997) pick out the dispositional or behavioral aspect. I take all of these accounts to be partially correct. As my examples show, they are wrong in taking their single condition to be either necessary or sufficient. Since the cluster account includes all these elements of desire, I do not discuss these other competing accounts at length, but instead concentrate on the more recent neurophysical reductionist account.

[11] Arpaly and Schroeder (2014), p. 97.
[12] A summary of their positions can be found in Annette Baier (1986).

by postulation, but there would no longer be undesired but pleasant surprises. We have all experienced such fortunate cases.

If being constituted as a reward is not sufficient for being the object of a desire, we can nevertheless cheerfully add this condition to the cluster of criterial properties in my account. It will be the least obvious because least observable member from the first and third person viewpoints. But, perhaps surprisingly, this is in a sense one reason why Arpaly and Schroeder focus on it. In their view it allows them to causally explain the occurrences of the other elements by appeal to desire itself, giving the account a major advantage in terms of explanatory power. Let us return to this claim.

Explanatory Power

Contingency

Reductionists identify (but do not define) desire as what causes behavioral dispositions and pleasure in its satisfaction, and they identify this cause in the brain with the operation of the reward system. The first argument for this account appeals to the claimed contingent relation between desire and its effects. Since the relation of this cause to its effects is, as is always the case with causes according to a Humean account, contingent, one can explain both pleasurable feelings and behavior by appeal to desire and its satisfaction. These explanations seem perfectly in order, but they would not be according to Humeans if desire were defined by or constituted by the cluster of properties, including both behavioral dispositions and pleasurable thoughts or feelings, included in my analysis. "Why did he do it?" "Because he was disposed to," is like "Why did the pill put him to sleep?" "Because it was sleep inducing"—seemingly no explanations at all. Explanatory power is a test of a good theory, and reductionists claim that only their account of desire has such power.

Before replying directly to this argument, one might respond again to their overall position by reiterating that, at least from the first person viewpoint, we do not make a causal inference to a hidden brain state when ascribing desires to ourselves. We do not typically ascribe desires to ourselves in order to predict or explain our behavior, although we might revise such ascriptions when our actions surprise us. Even in the case of reacting to others, we respond directly to their desires and emotions without making inferences to brain states: what we seem to respond to in interacting with others are not the effects of emotions and desires, but perceived emotions and desires in behavior, facial expressions, manners of speaking, etc. In ordinary contexts of social interaction, we do not explain or predict each other's behavior by appealing to brain states. But the analogy with water, while very imperfect overall, could be of use in responding to this point. Unless we are in a chemistry class, we do not infer a hidden chemical compound in identifying water. But water is that compound. So might desire be a state in the brain that releases dopamine, however we typically identify and react to it.

We therefore do better to reply to this argument directly. The first reply is that, despite examples involving dormativity and the Humean claim that all causes are contingently related to their effects, that a state involves causal powers essentially or criterially does not preclude causal explanations of its effects by appeal to the state or its parts. Actions essentially involve reasons, but reasons must be causes of the actions if we are to distinguish the reasons for which an agent acted from those she had but which did not affect the actions. And we appeal to the reasons in explaining the actions. An explanation of an action simply in terms of a disposition might be trivial, but to explain that a person acted as he did because he desired to may not be, contracting with his being forced to, his acting out of habit, and so on. Such contrasts would hold even if desires were essentially motivational.

Furthermore, if desires contain multiple elements, then, as is true in general, parts can explain each other, parts can explain the whole, and the whole can explain the parts, even if the elements are conceptually related to the whole. "Why did he feel like running away?" "Why did he tremble?" "Because he was afraid." "Why does that bird have webbed feet?" "Because it's a duck." "Why does he judge it to be good?" "Because he finds the thought of it pleasant." "Why does she desire it?" "Because the thought of it pleases her." "Why does that figure have four equal sides?" "Because it's a square" (and vice versa). All these are legitimate explanations in certain contexts, and they can be causal explanations when the parts of the whole cause other parts. So to explain an action by appeal to a disposition to that action might be trivial in most contexts, but to appeal to the other elements of desire to causally explain the disposition and the action will most often not be trivial, even if these elements constitute criteria for having desires.

Finally, the same counterargument applies to rewards. "Why will that cookie be a reward for her?" "Because she desires it." "Why does he want that cup?" "Because it is used as a reward for winning." Again these are legitimate causal explanations, but they could not be according to the argument we are considering for the reward system analysis. These explanations need not be trivial, as they would be on the reward account of desire. It therefore lacks this explanatory power on its own terms. This lack is easily overlooked and might seem a small price to pay, but only because, as noted, being a reward is the least prominent aspect of being desired. That is why it seems more important to be able to causally explain the other elements of the cluster by appeal to desire itself. But in all these cases what we typically do, even if only implicitly, is to explain some of the elements by appeal to the others.

In regard to the element of pleasure, Arpaly and Schroeder offer an additional but closely related argument why it cannot be conceptually linked to or constitutive of desire. As noted, they claim that pleasure represents change in desire satisfaction (relative to expectation). They write: "Since pleasure and displeasure represent desires, they cannot be even partially constitutive of desire any more than a picture of Marie Curie can be even partially constitutive of Marie Curie."[13] Although it greatly oversimplifies, as is obvious from my first chapter, I will not quarrel with their analysis of pleasure here, but the analogy is again misleading, and the general conclusion does not follow. Facial expressions represent emotions, but they are also criterial for or partly constitutive of emotions as well as being caused by them. A cluster analysis in which certain of the criterial elements cause others once more accounts for this possibility.

We can represent a three-dimensional cube by drawing a two-dimensional square, that is, a figure having 90 degree angles and equal sides. These features then represent the cube and are partially constitutive of its being the shape that it is. Thus pleasure can be criterial for desire while also representing it. And we have seen that there is no advantage of the reward system account over the cluster analysis in causally explaining behavioral dispositions, resultant actions, and pleasurable thoughts or feelings.

---

[13] Arpaly and Schroeder (2014), p. 124.

The cognitive element

There is a major disadvantage to the reductionist account in that the reward system does not explain or include the major cognitive aspect of desire, positive evaluative judgment. For Arpaly and Schroeder desires are noncognitive attitudes.[14] Their cognitive effects are limited to the ways they influence learning, attention, and memory. Since the reward system does not directly influence judgment or belief, evaluative judgment must be omitted from their account of desire. They seem to admit the disadvantage here in admitting that "beliefs about (or perceptions of) value (or reasons) must be at the center of motivational psychology," while noting that the reward system "does not appear to be required for, or to realize, ordinary thinking about values."[15] In my view values, which ultimately produce one's practical reasons, equate with or derive from one's deeper or more central desires, those that connect with many others, and evaluative judgment within a particular desire typically indicates its centrality or connection with those deeper desires.[16]

In order for desire to guide action toward realization of its object in an intelligent way, the desire must not simply push the agent mechanically or by an urge, but pull by an evaluative judgment of the object's worth. Desire aims not only at its own satisfaction but typically at its conception of the good. Such evaluative judgments are normally the best indicators of one's strongest reasons for acting. The claim that desires are non-cognitive attitudes, coupled with an exclusive focus on reward-based or reinforcement learning, suggests a Skinnerian theory of behavior that oversimplifies the ways that sophisticated desires, including desires for such abstract objects as justice or world peace, interact with beliefs to produce actions aimed at long range collective goals.

Deep intrinsic desires constitute various states of affairs as reasons. What makes them reasons is not that their representation or realization releases a signal in the brain in the form of dopamine, but that they become objects of instrumental motivation, indications of ways to satisfy the deeper desires, and sources of pleasure. It would be a sobering thought at best that to have a reason to pursue x is to have dopamine

---

[14] Arpaly and Schroeder (2014), p. 215.
[15] Arpaly and Schroeder (2014), p. 295.
[16] See Goldman (2009), ch. 3, section 3.

secreted in one's brain at the representation of x, and that this secretion occurs independently of any positive evaluation of x. It may be true that the satisfaction of desire reinforces behavior chemically, but this must be only part of the story.

The argument that desires themselves are more complex and cognitive than reductionists allow is, however, better stated in more concrete terms appealing to the phenomenology of conflicts within desires. In instances of weak will, a felt urge overwhelms the evaluative judgmental component. I know that I should not eat that cheesecake, but I can't resist it. In other cases in which will power is able to resist such an urge or temptation, it is the motivational force of the evaluative judgment that prevails over the felt urge. I know that I should finish writing this appendix instead of going out to play golf, and so I stay in. Since desire is a motivational state, this is not an ordinary belief opposing a desire, but a tension within motivation itself. One feels a tension within one's motivational state, the motivational force of the evaluative component being sometimes sufficient to prevail and preserve welfare. If this component has motivational force in itself, then it is a proper component of desire (accepting Hume's insight that desire can be effectively opposed only by desire). That it has such force is evidenced also by the fact that affect and behavioral disposition can be altered by such judgment; also by the fact that the normal feel of a desire is not simply negative, the feeling of yearning or lack, but positive, under the influence of pleasant images and positive evaluations.

For Arpaly and Schroeder, the case in which will power is able to prevail over an urge or felt temptation requires an additional desire: the desire to do what is best, which must combine with an ordinary belief about what is best in the circumstances.[17] This must presumably be a standing desire that is present in all people who are ever able to resist temptation. This again appears to be an ad hoc superfluous postulation similar to that of the standing desire for various pleasurable experiences considered earlier. But there is a worse problem with it, deriving from the fact that not all evaluative judgments have motivational force, as they would when combined with this standing desire. I judge that eating kale and drinking fish oil would be good for me overall without being

---

[17] Arpaly and Schroeder (2014), p. 260.

motivated at all to do so. But the standing desire to do what is best should produce that motivation that is absent. I simply do not have that standing desire, and I need not appeal to it to explain why I normally act on my strongest reasons reflecting my deepest desires at various times.

My conclusion for this section is that the cluster analysis provides a better account of the causal powers of desire than does the reward system analysis. The latter is not superior on predictive or explanatory grounds. It can predict behavior by appealing to contingent but typical causal relations to desires, which vary in strength as do rewards. But the cluster analysis has similar predictive power while also explaining rewards and evaluative judgments, as the reward system account cannot.

Neurophysical Reduction

The reward system is a discrete physical system in the brain, allowing a neat one-to-one mapping of the folk psychological type, desire, onto the neurophysiological type. The assumption of scientifically minded philosophers of mind is that psychology will ultimately reduce to neurophysiology. If causal explanations all appeal ultimately to physical processes, this reduction is at least an ideal aim of philosophers who want to resist the elimination of folk psychological concepts. Type reduction is the preferable alternative until shown to be impossible, in which case the assumption is that physicalists will have to settle for eliminativism as the outcome at the end of scientific inquiry. The reason reduction is preferable to elimination is that it provides an explanation for the noted great success of folk psychological categories in explanations and predictions of human behavior.

The fact that we socially interact so successfully when at present we have only these mentalistic categories by which to do so, together with the inaccessibility of brain states, indicates the future preservation of the folk psychological concepts. If there were not a single cause in the brain for what reductionists take to be the effects of desire, the reduction would not go through. A messy disjunction presumably will not do, because, like air, it will not be a natural kind. I questioned earlier whether we can really construe the reward system as a natural functional or psychological kind. Here I will question first whether Arpaly and Schroeder's reduction is as neat as they claim.

Incompleteness

The answer is no, it is not so neat: first, because there is no complete reduction to physical functional types in the brain. The reduction is incomplete because it appeals to mental representations in the brain without reducing or identifying these with physical functional types, and because the reward system reinforces actions, not physical movements, without again any attempt on their part to reduce the former. The reward system account holds that S desires p when the mental representation of p is constituted as a reward for S, reinforcing actions leading to the reward. In appealing to representations and actions, the reduction remains incomplete.

Eliminativists like Stich focused on beliefs and the multiple systems in the brain that produce verbal and nonverbal behavior that is taken to express them.[18] Stich argued that since beliefs fail to map onto common brain structures, they will not survive in mature science. Mental representations would presumably fall prey to the same argument, if it were sound. This produces a dilemma for the reward system reduction of desire. On the one hand, if the Stich argument is sound, if reductions require single or discrete systems in the brain as underlying causes, and if beliefs and mental representations generally fail to map onto such systems, then not only would the reduction of desire remain incomplete, but its future completion would not be forthcoming. On the other hand, if an argument of this type for elimination is not sound, then, as I will argue further below, there is no advantage to a neat reduction in the first place.

What is true of mental representations in this regard is also true of actions, which, of course, are multiply realizable in physical movements and so cross-classify them. In addition, actions are explained by reasons, and, as I argued earlier, the appeal to evaluative judgments, missing from the reward system's account of desires, might be required for identifying reasons, even if reasons themselves are reducible. Davidson's admonition against attempting to reduce the realm of the rational to that of the physical begins to look more applicable and damaging here. In any case, the very partial reduction of desires offered by reductionists now looks like a very small step toward completing what may well be impossible to

[18] Stephen Stich (1983).

complete. Even a complete reduction of desire would seem irrelevant if we cannot similarly reduce belief and action, since desires produce actions only in conjunction with beliefs, and psychologists want to know why agents desire, believe, and act as they do.

Relations to other mental states

A second reason why their reduction is not neat is that the reward system account of desire fails to reveal the close structural similarities between intrinsic desires, the focus of the account, and other mental states, most obviously instrumental desires. There is a reason why we conceptualize instrumental desires as desires, and the cluster account captures that reason. Instrumental desires contain all the elements of the cluster except the pleasant thoughts and the constitution of the object as a reward. An ordinary trip to the dentist is not rewarding or pleasurable, nor is its representation beforehand, but it is instrumentally desired: one is disposed or motivated to go, judges it good to go, and directs attention in that direction. Since the reward system is not directly involved, there is no indication in that account of desire why this is a desire.[19] In fact, if the mapping of desires in general becomes messy at this point, we might expect the general concept of desire to be eliminated from mature science according to the Stich-type argument summarized earlier. A neat physiological account of intrinsic desire has little attraction if combined with a messy account of desire.

The reward account also fails to reveal the similarities between desires and emotions, as the cluster account does. Emotions are again closely structurally (in terms of the cluster of criterial properties) and functionally related to desires, although the areas of the brain involved are distinct. Unlike in the case of desires, we saw that it has become standard for psychologists to give cluster accounts of emotions.[20] Thus a paradigm case such as fear, universally identified as an emotion by test subjects, represents its object as dangerous or threatening, involves a disposition to flee or avoid the object, and produces bodily changes as well as sensations that may be interpreted as perceptions of those changes.

---

[19] Schroeder (2004) indicates the additional structures involved in generating instrumental desires, p. 154.

[20] Early proponents of this sort of analysis were Fehr and Russell (1984). Even Arpaly and Schroeder (2014) appear to endorse this sort of analysis for emotions, p. 216.

Like desires, prototypical emotions involve evaluative-judgmental, motivational or dispositional, and affective or sensational aspects. Less prototypical instances can again lack any one or two of these facets, and any of them can be present in the absence of emotion. While structurally similar in the terms of the cluster accounts, emotions and desires also play similar but distinct functional roles. The functional role of desires is to prompt actions based on reasons that indicate how to satisfy those desires, while the functional role of paradigmatic basic emotions is to displace ordinary calculation based on reasons for more rapid reactions. Emotions are irruptive motivational states, while desires are ordinary motivational states.

If desire is located in the reward system of the brain, and we look to the neurophysiological grounds of emotion, these close relations will not easily reveal themselves. In regard to the neural causes of emotions, as mentioned earlier, Paul Griffiths has advocated their elimination from scientific explanation on the usual ground that there is no single causal mechanism behind the various states that we ordinarily classify as emotions.[21] According to him, the concept of emotion is not scientifically proper because the concept is not explanatorily unified in best causal explanations. I have emphasized that if, by contrast, the alleged neat reduction of desire according to the reward system account is to be of any advantage, this type of argument must have bite. Only if we require a single neural cause of the properties of desire included in the cluster in order to avoid elimination in scientific explanations of the concept (and so no explanation for its present ubiquitous and successful use), will this requirement support the analysis offered by Arpaly and Schroeder.

Turning to another related state, in the chapter on happiness I did not characterize its opposite: depression. Some psychologists hold that depressed people are less inclined to do things that they intrinsically desire, while others hold that depressed people lose many of their desires.[22] In order to decide between these alternatives, we would not, I presume, best look to the activity of the reward system. In fact the cluster analysis indicates that we might not need to choose between them, that they may be simply alternative ways of describing the same situation. What typically happens in depression is that the subject loses

[21] Griffiths (1997).   [22] Arpaly and Schroeder (2014), p. 297.

the disposition to act, one aspect of desire, but retains the evaluative judgmental aspect.[23] Given that some elements of the cluster are missing while others remain, we can describe this situation either as loss of desire or as loss of inclination to act on desire. We have a borderline case, well captured by the cluster analysis.

Need we reduce in order to preserve?

We can then question finally whether such a neat reduction is necessary in order to avoid elimination of the concept of desire from a mature science of psychology. The decades old debate regarding the future of folk psychology shows this requirement to be at the least highly questionable. The simple general moral that I want to extract from that debate, which was extensive but never focused on desire, is that the whole point of a functional analysis depends on its multiple realizability at the lower level, its cross-classification of types at that level. This is again why we speak of actions and not physical movements when explaining how people behave. The same holds true for purely physical or psychological functional types; as I mentioned earlier, the reward system itself, functionally defined, is multiply physically realizable. That guns are not type reducible to molecular structures explains why ultimate explanations of how various people were murdered will still mention the use of guns.

In general, when a particular effect would have resulted from any one of a set of particular causes, conceptualized as a type that has the set as its extension, the best explanation for why the effect occurred on a particular occasion will typically appeal to the broader concept. If a batter in baseball cannot hit a curve ball, then the best explanation for his having struck out is that he was thrown a curve, not that the ball had the particular arc that it did have. This point was not emphasized in these terms by defenders of folk psychology,[24] but it is of most relevance here since it implies that the descriptive, explanatory, and predictive usefulness of any functional concept does not depend on its type reduction to a lower level type. In fact, just the opposite appears to true. The indispensability of any functional type would more likely depend on the lack of such a reduction.

---

[23] For expansion and defense of this description, see Goldman (2009), ch. 3, section 2.
[24] But compare Jonathan Bennett (1991) and Simon Blackburn (1991).

Thus, even if the reduction of desire to a purely psychophysical functional type or natural kind were neat, this would not constitute an argument for the use of the reduction in explanations. Reductionists take their reduction to save the concept of desire from elimination in mature psychological science, equated with neurological science, but this implies their sharing with eliminativists the thesis that elimination from mature explanations is the alternative to a neat mapping. Ironically, the thesis is that absent the prospect of such a mapping, we should *believe* there are no beliefs, and *want* to replace the concept of desire. I share with defenders of other folk psychological concepts the rejection of this thesis. When we ascribe desires to others, it is not to posit a unitary state of the brain, but to predict and explain how they will act, what feelings they will express, how they evaluate various states of affairs, and so on. If we are minimally sophisticated, we will assume that some neural processes causally underlie these psychological states, but we need not be more specific than that. Finally, just as we ascribe desires to animals, we would do so in the case of aliens exhibiting parts of the cluster as well, in their case without assuming that their learning is reward-based or that their brains are even structurally like ours.

Concluding Remarks

Some final more general and speculative comments. What reductionists in regard to desire offer is a hybrid functional reduction in partial neurophysical terms, appealing to the release of dopamine in the brain, but again appealing as well to representation and action. Ultimately the logical outcome of the reductionist impulse is the reduction of neurophysiology itself to chemistry and physics. Reference to dopamine might remain in this final account, along with electrical impulses across nerve endings and movements of muscles. But even were these physical events observable or immediately inferable from observations of behavior, the forthcoming explanations and predictions in these terms would be too fine grained to be of use to interactions among humans like us. If we had a description of the nerve impulses and muscle movements involved in an act of murder, we would have to translate back to motives and actions in order to convict the murderer. Once more the broader concepts of beliefs, desires, and curve balls would seem to be more functional in a human world, if such a world survived, not to mention the reasons to which we appeal in all moral and legal matters.

Certainly from the first person viewpoint, whatever is happening in my brain now, I could not be convinced that I don't want to end this discussion and go out to play golf. (Having made it through this book, you are welcome to join me if you are ever in the vicinity of Williamsburg.)

Bibliography

Abramson, P. R. and Pinkerton, S. D. (2002). *With Pleasure: Thoughts on the Nature of Human Sexuality*. Oxford: Oxford University Press.

Arpaly, N. and Schroeder, T. (2014). *In Praise of Desire*. Oxford: Oxford University Press.

Badhwar, N. (2014). *Well-Being: Happiness in a Worthwhile Life*. Oxford: Oxford University Press.

Baier, A. (1986). The ambiguous limits of desire. In Marks, J. (Ed.), *The Ways of Desire*. Chicago: Precedent.

Baier, K. (2008). The meaning of life. In Klemke, E. D. and Cahn, S. M. (Eds.), *The Meaning of Life*. Oxford: Oxford University Press.

Bates, J. E., Goodnight, J. A., and Fite, J. E. (2008). Temperament and emotion. In Lewis, M., Haviland-Jones, J. M., and Barrett, L. F. (Eds.), *Handbook of Emotions*. New York: Guilford.

Bennett, J. (1991). Folk-psychological explanations. In Greenwood, J. (Ed.), *The Future of Folk Psychology*. Cambridge: Cambridge University Press.

Bishop, M. (2015). *The Good Life*. Oxford: Oxford University Press.

Blackburn, S. (1991). Losing your mind. In Greenwood, J. (Ed.), *The Future of Folk Psychology*. Cambridge: Cambridge University Press.

Bloom, P. (2010). *How Pleasure Works*. New York: W. W. Norton.

Bloomfield, P. (2014). *The Virtues of Happiness*. Oxford: Oxford University Press.

Bradley, B. (2007). A paradox for some theories of welfare. *Philosophical Studies*, 133.

Brandt, R. (1979). *A Theory of the Good and the Right*. Oxford: Clarendon.

Campbell, S. M. (2016). The concept of well-being. In Fletcher, G. (Ed.), *The Routledge Handbook of Philosophy of Well-Being*. New York: Routledge.

Chang, R. (2004). Can desires provide reasons for actions? In Wallace, R. J. (Ed.), *Reason and Value*. Oxford: Clarendon.

Clore, G. L. and Ortony, A. (2008). How cognition shapes affect into emotion. In Lewis, M., Haviland-Jones, J. M., and Barrett, L. F. (Eds.), *Handbook of Emotions*. New York: Guilford.

Cohen, J. (2005). Colors, functions, realizers, roles. *Philosophical Topics*, 33.

Cottingham, J. (2003). *On the Meaning of Life*. London: Routledge.

Crisp, R. (2006). *Reasons and the Good*. Oxford: Clarendon.

Darwall, S. (2002). *Welfare and Rational Care*. Princeton: Princeton University Press.

Dworkin, R. (1986). *Law's Empire*. Cambridge, MA: Harvard University Press.

Fehr, B. and Russell, J. (1984). Concept of emotion viewed from a prototype perspective. *Journal of Experimental Psychology: General*, 113.

Feldman, F. (2004). *Pleasure and the Good Life*. Oxford: Clarendon.

Feldman, F. (2010). *What is This Thing Called Happiness?* Oxford: Oxford University Press.

Fletcher, G. (2016). Objective list theory. In Fletcher, G. (Ed.), *The Routledge Handbook of Philosophy of Well-being*. New York: Routledge.

Frankfurt, H. G. (2004). *The Reasons of Love*. Princeton: Princeton University Press.

Fredrickson, B. L. and Cohn, M. A. (2008). Positive emotions. In Lewis, M., Haviland-Jones, J. M., and Barrett, L. F. (Eds.), *Handbook of Emotions*. New York: Guilford.

Frijda, N. (2008). The psychologists' point of view. In Lewis, M., Haviland-Jones, J. M., and Barrett, L. F. (Eds.), *Handbook of Emotions*. New York: Guilford.

Frijda, N. (2010). On the nature and function of pleasure. In Kingelbach, M. L. and Berridge, K. C. (Eds.), *Pleasures of the Brain*. Oxford: Oxford University Press.

Gaut, B. (2000). "Art" as a cluster concept. In Carroll, N. (Ed.), *Theories of Art Today*. Madison, WI: University of Wisconsin Press.

Georgiadis, J. R. and Kortekaas, R. (2010). The sweetest taboo: A functional neuro-biology of human sexuality in relation to pleasure. In Kingelbach, M. L. and Berridge, K. C. (Eds.), *Pleasures of the Brain*. Oxford: Oxford University Press.

Gert, D. (n.d.). Pleasure and pain. In an unpublished manuscript on human nature.

Gibbard, A. (1990). *Wise Choices, Apt Feelings*. Cambridge, MA: Harvard University Press.

Goldman, A. H. (1977). Plain sex. *Philosophy & Public Affairs*, 6.

Goldman, A. H. (1988). *Moral Knowledge*. London: Routledge.

Goldman, A. H. (1995). *Aesthetic Value*. Boulder, CO: Westview.

Goldman, A. H. (2007). Desire, depression, and rationality. *Philosophical Psychology*, 20.

Goldman, A. H. (2009). *Reasons from Within*. Oxford: Oxford University Press.

Goldman, A. H. (2010). Is moral motivation rationally required? *The Journal of Ethics*, 14.

Goldman, A. H. (2013). *Philosophy and the Novel*. Oxford: Oxford University Press.

Goldman, A. H. (2017). What desires are, and are not. *Philosophical Studies*, 174.

Griffin, J. (1986). *Well-Being*. Oxford: Oxford University Press.

Griffiths, P. (1997). *What Emotions Really Are*. Chicago: University of Chicago Press.

Gross, J. J. (2008). Emotion regulation. In Lewis, M., Haviland-Jones, J. M., and Barrett, L. F. (Eds.), *Handbook of Emotions*. New York: Guilford.

Haybron, D. M. (2013). *Happiness*. Oxford: Oxford University Press.

Heathwood, C. (2011). Preferentism and self-sacrifice. *Pacific Philosophical Quarterly*, 92.

Heathwood, C. (2016). Desire-fulfilment theory. In Fletcher, G. (Ed.), *The Routledge Handbook of Philosophy of Well-being*. New York: Routledge.

Hume, D. (1985). The skeptic. In *Essays*. Indianapolis: Liberty Fund.

Ito, T. A. and Cacioppo, J. T. (1999). The psychophysiology of utility appraisals. In Kahneman, D., Diener, E., and Schwarz, N. (Eds.), *Well-Being: The Foundations of Hedonic Psychology*. New York: Russell Sage Foundation.

Kahneman, D. (1999). Objective happiness. In Kahneman, D., Diener, E., and Schwarz, N. (Eds.), *Well-Being: The Foundations of Hedonic Psychology*. New York: Russell Sage Foundation.

Katz, L. (2005). Review of *Three Faces of Desire*, *Notre Dame Philosophical Reviews* [electronic journal], Sep. 9.

Kierkegaard, S. (1959). *Either/Or*, vol. 1. Garden City, NY: Anchor.

Kringelbach, M. L. (2010). The hedonic brain: A functional neuroanatomy of human pleasure. In Kingelbach, M. L. and Berridge, K. C. (Eds.), *Pleasures of the Brain*. Oxford: Oxford University Press.

Kubovy, M. (1999). On the pleasures of the mind. In Kahneman, D., Diener, E., and Schwarz, N. (Eds.), *Well-Being: The Foundations of Hedonic Psychology*. New York: Russell Sage Foundation.

Lamarque, P. (2007). On the distance between literary narratives and real life narratives. In Hutto, D. (Ed.), *Narrative and Understanding Persons*. Cambridge: Cambridge University Press.

Leknes, S. and Tracey, I. (2010). Pain and pleasure: Masters of mankind. In Kingelbach, M. L. and Berridge, K. C. (Eds.), *Pleasures of the Brain*. Oxford: Oxford University Press.

Lewis, M. (2008). The emergence of human emotions. In Lewis, M., Haviland-Jones, J. M., and Barrett, L. F. (Eds.), *Handbook of Emotions*. New York: Guilford.

Leyton, M. (2010). The neurobiology of desire. In Kingelbach, M. L. and Berridge, K. C. (Eds.), *Pleasures of the Brain*. Oxford: Oxford University Press.

Mackie, J. L. (1977). *Inventing Right and Wrong*. New York: Penguin.

Mele, A. (2003). *Motivation and Agency*. Oxford: Oxford University Press.

Metz, T. (2013). *Meaning in Life*. Oxford: Oxford University Press.

Millgram, E. (1997). *Practical Induction*. Cambridge, MA: Harvard University Press.

Moore, A. (2000). Objective human goods. In Crisp, R. and Hooker, B. (Eds.), *Well-Being and Morality*. Oxford: Clarendon.

Mulnix, J. W. and Mulnix, M. J. (2015). *Happy Lives, Good Lives*. Peterborough, Ontario: Broadview.

Nagel, T. (1971). The absurd. *The Journal of Philosophy*, 63.

Nagel, T. (2002). Sexual perversion. In Sobel, A. (Ed.), *Philosophy of Sex*. Lanham, MD: Rowman & Littlefield.

Nettle, D. (2005). *Happiness*. Oxford: Oxford University Press.

Niedenthal, P. M. (2008). Emotion concepts. In Lewis, M., Haviland-Jones, J. M., and Barrett, L. F. (Eds.), *Handbook of Emotions*. New York: Guilford.

Nielsen, K. (2008). Linguistic philosophy and "the meaning of life." In Klemke, E. D. and Cahn, S. M. (Eds.), *The Meaning of Life*. Oxford: Oxford University Press.

Nozick, R. (1989). *The Examined Life*. New York: Simon and Schuster.

Panksepp, J. (2008). The affective brain and core consciousness. In Lewis, M., Haviland-Jones, J. M., and Barrett, L. F. (Eds.), *Handbook of Emotions*. New York: Guilford.

Rawls, J. (1971). *A Theory of Justice*. Cambridge, MA: Harvard University Press.

Raz, J. (1999). *Engaging Reason*. Oxford: Oxford University Press.

Ryle, G. (1949). *The Concept of Mind*. New York: Barnes & Noble.

Scanlon, T. (1998). *What We Owe to Each Other*. Cambridge, MA: Harvard University Press.

Schecterman, M. (2007). Stories, lives, and basic survival. In Hutto, D. (Ed.), *Narrative and Understanding Persons*. Cambridge: Cambridge University Press.

Schooler, J. W. and Mauss, I. B. (2010). To be happy and to know it. In Kingelbach, M. L. and Berridge, K. C. (Eds.), *Pleasures of the Brain*. Oxford: Oxford University Press.

Schroeder, T. (2004). *Three Faces of Desire*. Oxford: Oxford University Press.

Schueler, G. F. (1995). *Desire*. Cambridge, MA: MIT Press.

Sidgwick, H. (1907). *The Methods of Ethics*. London: Macmillan.

Skelton, A. (2016). Children's well-being: A philosophical analysis. In Fletcher, G. (Ed.), *The Routledge Handbook of Philosophy of Well-Being*. New York: Routledge.

Skow, B. (2009). Preferentism and the paradox of desire. *Journal of Ethics and Social Philosophy*, 3.

Sobel, D. (2016). *From Valuing to Value*. Oxford: Oxford University Press.

Solomon, R. (2002). Sexual paradigms. In Sobel, A. (Ed.), *Philosophy of Sex*. Lanham, MD: Rowman & Littlefield.

Solomon, R. (2007). *True to Our Feelings*. Oxford: Oxford University Press.

Stein, N. L., Hernandez, M. W., and Trabasso, T. (2008). Advances in modeling emotion and thought. In Lewis, M., Haviland-Jones, J. M., and Barrett, L. F. (Eds.), *Handbook of Emotions*. New York: Guilford.

Stich, S. (1983). *From Folk Psychology to Cognitive Science*. Cambridge, MA: MIT Press.

Sumner, L. W. (1996). *Welfare, Happiness, and Ethics*. Oxford: Clarendon.

Szasz, T. S. (1975). *Pain and Pleasure*. New York: Basic Books.

Tatarkiewicz, W. (1976). *Analysis of Happiness*, E. Rothert and D. Zielinskn (Trans.). Warsaw: Polish Scientific Publishers.

Taylor, R. (2008). The meaning of life. In Klemke, E. D. and Cahn, S. (Eds.), *The Meaning of Life*. Oxford: Oxford University Press.

Tiberius, V. (2015). Prudential value. In Hirose, I. and Olson, J. (Eds.), *The Oxford Handbook of Value Theory*. Oxford: Oxford University Press.

Twain, M. (1994). The good little boy who did not prosper. The bad little boy who led a charmed life. In Quirk, T. (Ed.), *Tales, Speeches, Essays, and Sketches*. New York: Penguin.

Walton, K. (1990). *Mimesis as Make-Believe*. Cambridge, MA: Harvard University Press.

Williams, B. (2001). Internal and external reasons. In Millgram, E. (Ed.), *Varieties of Practical Reasoning*. Cambridge, MA: MIT Press.

Wittgenstein, L. (1958). *Philosophical Investigations*, G. E. M. Anscombe (Trans.). New York: Macmillan.

Wolf, S. (1997). Happiness and meaning: two aspects of the good life. *Social Philosophy and Policy*, 24.

Wolf, S. (2014). Susan Wolf on meaning in life. In Edmonds, D. and Warburton, N. (Eds.), *Philosophy Bites Again*. Oxford: Oxford University Press.

Woodard, C. (2013). Classifying theories of welfare. *Philosophical Studies*, 165.

Zahavi, D. (2007). Self and other. In Hutto, D. (Ed.), *Narrative and Understanding Persons*. Cambridge: Cambridge University Press.

Index